CAITLÍN MATTHEWS is one of the few people to have explored the Celtic vision and seership traditions from both source materials and also from personal practice. Her seership programme *Augury and Inspiration: Celtic Divination from Nature* has been given all over the world. She is a founder of FÍOS, the Foundation for Inspirational and Oracular Studies, dedicated to the oral and unwritten arts of divination, ancestral ritual, augury and oracular vision. She is the author of over 60 books.

To study with Caitlín Matthews, *see* www.hallowquest. org.uk for details of her courses, books and events.

A Selection of Books by Caitlín Matthews

Celtic Devotional
Celtic Myths and Legends
Celtic Book of the Dead
Encyclopedia of Celtic Wisdom
Singing the Soul Back Home
King Arthur's Raid on the Underworld
Mabon and Guardians of Celtic Britain
Storyworld

CELTIC
VISIONS

Seership, Omens
and Dreams
of the Otherworld

CAITLÍN MATTHEWS

WATKINS PUBLISHING
LONDON

This edition first published in the UK and USA 2012 by
Watkins Publishing, Sixth Floor, Castle House,
75–76 Wells Street, London W1T 3QH

1 3 5 7 9 10 8 6 4 2

Designed and typeset by Jerry Goldie Graphic Design

Printed and bound in China by Imago

British Library Cataloguing-in-Publication Data Available
Library of Congress Cataloging-in-Publication Data Available

ISBN: 978-1-78028-111-7

www.watkinspublishing.co.uk

Distributed in the USA and Canada by Sterling Publishing Co., Inc.
387 Park Avenue South, New York, NY 10016-8810

For information about custom editions, special sales, premium and
corporate purchases, please contact Sterling Special Sales
Department at 800-805-5489 or specialsales@sterlingpub.com

This book is dedicated to my son,
Emrys Matthews: may the *gléfiosa*
shine upon his way!

ACKNOWLEDGEMENTS

I thank Dwina Murphy Gibb for conversations about the charm, Robert Moss for his insights into dreaming, and RJ Stewart for his skilful opening of faery doors. As ever, thanks to John for graciously holding the space and to my students for being the sounding boards of these teachings.

Contents

Kindling the Bright Knowledge

What we see and what we imagine has one connected life. For the people of the ancient Celtic world, seership opened windows into the otherworld. It awakened the essence of true vision and wisdom, which was known by the poets as the *gléfiosa* or 'the bright knowledge'.

Seership is a means of understanding the connections between the two sides of reality: both the physical, manifest world that is perceptible by our everyday senses, as well as the invisible, unmanifest world that we perceive with our inner senses. When seers go seeking, they expand their consciousness to perceive the wider reality of the whole. At one time this skill was more commonly shared by our ancestors who had a strongly developed instinct, but there have always been specialists whose senses were yet more attuned to that wider reality; individuals who could sense from the movement or location of animals, who smelt the coming of a dangerous event or when a sickness augured certain death.

The primordial condition of the human soul is based upon metaphors of perception: this primal language of the soul is received by the inner senses and conveyed primarily through the images and metaphors of storytelling, song and poetry. When viewing a landscape, the seer saw not just the hills or rivers, but a living world in which the sound of the waters, the wind through the trees and the movements of animals were meaningful. Each place had its own memories where certain teachings or stories might be remembered. A land feature thus had power to reconnect the physical and unseen sides of reality, becoming a threshold where past, present and future fused into a single focus for knowing and understanding. A hill or a well had its spirit that was a living witness.

That we have fallen out of such a way of understanding the living world is evident: we rush to work unaware of the spirit of a noble birch tree that stands by the wayside, we pass unseeing through an area once famous for a battle, we ignore the ancestral wisdom that rises up in us. Our instincts have been tuned down, our insights dulled from too much electronic interface and our inspirations ignored because we don't live in a society that validates the gifts of seership or vision.

Some people are born with the 'second sight', which in Scots Gaelic is called *an da shealleadh*, literally meaning 'the two seeings'. Those in possession of the second sight perceive not only the physical semblance of a person or an event, but also its spiritual aspect as well. In an age that welcomes all kinds of signs and wonders, it should be remembered that the second sight was, and still is, an unwelcome gift for those who possess it, for it comes unbidden and can seldom be ignored or removed, only 'tuned down'. Seers do not boast of their skill because the responsibility for their perceptions is too heavy.

Diviners' skills were pragmatically sought out to find lost people or animals that had strayed, to discover news of far-travelling relatives or those who went into battle in an age with no instant means of communication. The interpretive skills of the seer might be welcome in times of need or very unwelcome indeed as when the poor Brahan Seer dared to speak the truth to a powerful lady and was killed for his temerity.

Methods of Celtic seership and vision have been my study for many years, both from written sources as well as from oral transmission and personal practice. With many students worldwide, I've explored how these methods can work today. The teaching of these skills has largely concentrated on enabling and recognizing the natural perceptions that everyone poten-tially possesses. Many people have discovered that their vision can also be fruitful, helpful and accurate. Practice over many years grows confidence and underscores the validity of the evidence. Seership is an inborn gift, but vision is a skill that can be reawakened within us by patient observation and faithful practice, by stillness, and the absence of stimulus or interruption. By slowing down, carrying a question patiently within our hearts, we can consider the evidence of our heightened senses and the verification of our dreams.

I have chosen to look at Celtic seership and visionary traditions across a wide range of material from different eras and traditions: the Gaelic strand is the strongest because there is more extant material. Many will complain that I have left out essential elements from this little book, but I have done my best with the space available.

In Chapter 1 we meet some of the seers and visionaries of the Celtic world, while in Chapter 2 we explore the second sight and the way of vision. These arise in the otherworld and are associated with faery, as we find in Chapter 3. In Chapter 4 we enter the Dark Cell where poets honed their visions and in Chapter 5 we investigate their prophetic skills. In Chapter 6 we go to the heart of fate and destiny that are the core discernments of vision. The art of prophecy is explored in Chapter 7, while in Chapter 8 we find the skill of reading omens and making divinations. Lastly, in Chapter 9, we open up the seer's worldview of sacred wholeness. Extracts and translations are sourced in the notes on p.213 while the glossary on p.225 gives the pronunciation of Celtic specialist words.

Ways to kindle the *gléfiosa* are given throughout this book. Be aware that they are merely signposts to wisdom, not the wisdom itself. *That* arrives in the still silence of darkness, shimmers on every hedgerow and sparkles at the water's edge. If you would kindle the bright knowledge for yourself, use these signposts and take the journey. Reading alone will not bring it any closer.

Do not expect experiences to match or echo what you know or suspect about Celtic beliefs. You perceive through your own cultural filters and background. Allow perceptions to arise through the natural array of your senses and be prepared to step out of the way of yourself, quieting your mind's chatter to experience what lies beyond. All methods presuppose that you practise these ways in a quiet and undisturbed space, without phones or music, and with respect. Assess your findings neutrally, without judgement or overrationalization. It is usual to think you are 'making things up', for about the first four years of practising. You will pass beyond this stage to understand and honour your experiences better.

This book will not make you into a seer, but it will help you become better attuned to your instincts, imagination, insight, and inspiration. How you use your findings ethically, without infringing the liberty or space of others, is a matter of courtesy that all seers honour. There are enough surveillance devices in the world without becoming one yourself. Obsessive practice and self-focus can be balanced by being of service in your community, where the needs of the world can always be found. Seers have ever been the servants of their community and it is this context that has kept seership and vision healthy.

Lastly, in your own reading, be aware that many instances of seership in Britain and Ireland may derive from even earlier ancestors who left only their earthworks or standing stones to tell us of their own visions. Where star, stone and earth touch, there too we may walk, wonder and reawaken.

Caitlín Matthews
Oxford
Samhain 2010 – Lady Day 2011

CHAPTER 1

Seers, Healers and Prophets

There was a tall man sitting next to me, and he dressed in grey, and after the Mass I asked him where he came from. 'From Tir-na-nOg,' says he. 'And where is that?' I asked him. 'It's not far from you,' he said; 'it's near the place where you live.'

Lady Augusta Gregory, *Visions and Beliefs in the West of Ireland*

The World of the Seers

The world we are exploring is a world you half remember. It draws not only upon the evidence of the five senses, but also upon the unseen world that meshes with it. It is not far from us, as the faery man tells us above. In order to apprehend this world, we must make some adjustments to our perception, for this is not just a subject you are reading about, but an experience into which you must also enter. The world of the seers, visionaries, healers and prophets of the Celtic peoples is much larger, broader, deeper than you have imagined.

Who are the seers? What kind of people are they? What is their purpose? In this chapter, we look at a variety of seers, named and unknown, to explore the context of their work. Throughout this book, we find seers who are professional walkers-between-the-worlds, as well as ordinary people who have the second sight; both are working as intermediaries between the seen and unseen worlds, which form one reality. They are pre-Christian and post-Christian seers, the latter kind often adhering to both levels of belief and fusing it into one practice. The work of seers varies according to their individual skills and standpoints. Some may see involuntarily or else may engage in procedures that invoke the vision. Some have spirit-allies who are of many kinds – animal, plant, ancestor, faery or spirit – some use traditional methods that rely on the signs of nature. Some, like the Scottish *frithirs* use divination or the seeing of omens to obtain answers; some have an instant knowledge while others, like the vision poets of the Gaelic world, trained in the houses of darkness, had their Three Illuminations (*see* Chapter 5) that are nearer to shamanism than to folk belief. Within these diverse categories there are seers who are healers or prophets, druids, saints, poor women and noblewomen. Seership is a skill that arises in every walk of life.

The primary purpose of intentional seership was, and is, practical: to find lost objects, animals and people; to uncover mysteries that cannot be solved by ordinary means; to look beyond the present time and place into the timeless vision to see what is, was or will be. Unintentional seership, as in the visions of those with second sight, reveal premonitions of events to come or visions of what has already happened elsewhere at distance. Both kinds of seership set the possessor apart from others, sometimes engendering fear, avoidance and hatred as much as awe and respect for such powers. Yet seership is primarily used for, and in, the community; a role that brings its own difficulties in different ages.

Wherever modernist views of the West have penetrated in the world, subjects like seership, faeries, the otherworld, vision and prophecy have little relevance. These topics only concern two kinds of groups: the religions that feel they alone have the correct view of the world and who condemn seership as 'the devil's tool', and those who turn toward ancestral beliefs and customs to find spiritual relevance for today. For our ancestors, it was a different matter. Their vision of the world was not sealed into one side of reality, but was understood by way of metaphor, dream and vision, as well as by the perceptions of the five senses. Let us meet some of these seers.

Druids and Saints

The influence of the druids lay at the heart of Celtic culture, for they were the arbiters who kept the world in balance by their wise judgements and pronouncements, by their philosophy and insight. Druids were not only associated with spiritual or other-worldly matters, but were prominent in law, philosophy, history, astronomy and many other skills. As the arbiters of wisdom and knowledge, druids in Celtic society were nearer to the Brahmins within Indian culture, or to the learned rabbis in Hasidic communities, as mediators and guides. The Bithynian teacher, Dio Chrysostom, wrote in the 1st century AD:

> The Celts appointed Druids, who likewise were versed in the art of seers and other forms of wisdom, without whom the kings were not permitted to adopt or plan any course, so that in effect it was these who ruled and the kings became their subordinates and instruments of their judgement.[1]

Individual druids had their own schools and followers, as well as being attached to noble households. It is possible that a certain section of society had a partial druidic education, in the same way that Buddhist boys in Thailand today still spend a period as monks before reverting to secular life again. For those who had a druidic vocation, the curriculum was much longer and was undertaken in secluded places. As the geographer, Pomponius Mela said of the druids:

> They teach many things to the noblest of the race in sequestered and remote places during twenty years, whether in a cave or in secluded groves.[2]

For the druids, the word of truth was paramount. They did not write down their teachings but maintained them orally, not from an inability to write, but so that teachings could be taught with the authority of the instructor, not open to the misinterpretation of any reader. Druidic training used question and answer as the primary means of learning, with all oral transmission coming through the route of repeated recitation. The old Irish words for 'teaching', 'instruction', and 'teacher' are derived from *for-cain*, which means 'singing by rote'. Druidic teaching was originally chanted, just as the Vedas are still chanted by Hindus. This is borne out by the metrical arrangement of texts that were transcribed in the Christian era into stanzas, making recitation easier. The examination of students was in the form of catechism, where the examiner began with *'Ceist'* or 'Question', and was always answered by the student's response of '*Ní ansa*', or 'not hard'.

Knowledge was often condensed into terse triads, for ease of memorization. The philosopher, Diogenes Laertius said that:

> Druids make their pronouncements by means of riddles and dark sayings, teaching that the gods must be worshipped, and no evil done, and manly behaviour maintained.[3]

These 'riddles and dark sayings' may refer to the triadic way in which they taught, for triads often embodied precedents of when a myth, story, a mode of moral behaviour or a tradition was first said. Knowledge and judgements were passed down by such precedents. For example, the very first occasion an honour price (an indemnity for an insult or injury) was demanded was in the time of Partholon, one of the first incomers to Ireland, when he left his wife alone with a servant and they committed adultery. Partholon then demanded his honour price, but his wife reckoned it was she who should demand it since it was the owner's responsibility to protect his property. And so the first ever judgement was uttered:

> Honey with a woman, milk with a cat;
> food with one generous, meat with a child;
> a wright within and an edged tool;
> one with another – it is a great risk.[4]

Keeping knowledge by means of oral tradition leads to a different mindset and outlook upon life. The word becomes paramount in honouring truth and upholding memory. When the ancient Irish Brehon laws came to be transcribed within the Christian era, it was asked what had preserved the teachings, and the answer given is:

> The joint memory of two seniors, the tradition from one ear to another, the composition of poets, the addition from the law of the letter, strength from the law of nature: for these are the three rocks by which the judgements of the world are supported.[5]

With the power of the word of truth to speed them, the incantations of druids were potent magic to shape reality. As the primacy of the druids and of the spoken word retreated under the new Christian regime, these incantations and word formulas became reworked into prayers, blessings and charms that people made to fend off illness and bad luck, and to protect their souls. The work of the keepers of memory also passed onto their successors, the clerics of the Irish Christian world, as we see from this 10th-century Irish text, the *Saltair na Rann*, a psalter about the creation of the world in verse. We hear that there are:

> The five things a wise person should know: the days of the solar month, the age of the moon, the tides of the sea, the day of the week, the calendar of holy days.[6]

Named druids are remembered only in Irish lore, but chief among them is Cathbad, the father of Conchobhor mac Nessa. Cathbad's foreknowledge tells him that the child in his wife's womb will be the king of Ulster if she gives birth to him on the morrow, but will be a mere nobody if he is born that day. While Nessa struggles not to give birth for a few hours more, Cathbad proclaims: 'Omen and portent are the same for him and for the king of the world.'[7] And he finally welcomes the baby with a prophecy: 'He will be a poet, he will be generous, he will lead warriors across the sea.' It is Cathbad who also proclaims the young hero, Cúchulainn.

Pre-Christian forms of seership are present, too, in the saints of the Celtic Christians, for the animistic beliefs of previous times did not depart when Christianity arrived. The consciousness of a culture sustains what is useful or necessary when it encounters change, often outwardly conforming while also inwardly turning to trusted and established spirits, as was still apparent in parts of Britain and Ireland until the 17th century when folk belief, healing practices and visionary experiences became the target of witch-hunts.[8]

An almost druidic foreknowledge of seership was accorded to the first abbot of Iona, St Columcille or Columba (d.597), whose life was composed by St Adomnan (d.704). Rather than being a sequential biography, the hagiography falls into three sections dealing with the prophetic revelations, the miracles, seership and the angelic apparitions of Columcille.

When visiting Clonmacnoise in Co. Offaly, Columcille picked out a boy called Ernene mac Crasen, who stood behind him, touching the hem of his cloak. Although the boy had little standing in the monastery, Columcille saw Ernene would become influential in the Church for his great eloquence. On another occasion, when Baíthene, Columcille's successor, proposed that the psalter just being painstakingly completed should be checked for errors, Columcille's seership established, without looking at the vellum pages, that only one 'i' had been omitted from the text. At his death, Columcille was mourned by Dallan Forgall, as one who was not only 'chief to the needy' and 'messenger of the Lord', but 'the seer who used to keep fears from us'. [9]

Prophets and Healers

Sometimes the seer is also a prophet, as in the case of the Brahan Seer, Coinnech Odhar or Sallow Kenneth, who came from the Isle of Lewis, and lived in the mid 17th century, though some of his legend seems to have its roots in the 16th century. He is said to have become a seer by practising a well-known charm: stealing an egg from a raven's nest, boiling it and returning it when cold to the nest. When the egg fails to hatch, the raven is said to go and seek for the Victory Stone and return it to the nest to encourage hatching; then the would-be seer steals the

Victory Stone, which endows victory in battle and the finder with prophecy. It is sometimes called 'the Little Stone of the Quests' because of its ability to find out what is unknown. At his life's end, Coinnech threw it into Loch Ussie, prophesying that it would, one day, be found in the belly of a fish, but this has not yet happened.

Another account told how, when Coinnech's mother was at the shieling (hill-grazing) watching the cattle one midnight, on a hill overlooking an ancient burial ground, she suddenly saw all the graves opening, and their occupants emerging from them and going off in all directions. After about an hour they returned and re-entered their tombs, and the graves closed over them again, except for one. With great courage she went to the grave and placed her distaff over it, because it was believed that, being of rowan wood, the spirit could not enter the grave while the distaff was there. Soon she saw a beautiful woman who rushed at her, demanding that she should remove her stick from the grave. Coinnech's mother refused to do this until the occupant of the grave told her why she came back so much later than the others. The spirit told her she was the daughter of a king of Norway and had drowned near the island; her body was recovered from the nearby beach. While she was released from the grave she had gone back to Norway to look at her old home. As a result of the woman's courage, the spirit gave her instructions on where to find a small, round, blue stone, which would empower her son to foresee future events. This she had to give to the boy.[10]

The Brahan Seer made many famous prophecies, including: 'The time will come when full-rigged ships will be seen sailing eastwards and westwards by the back of Tomnahurich.'[11] This prophecy prefigured the construction of the Caledonian Canal, begun in 1803. He also said that the Black Isle would come under the management of the fisherman of Avoch, a village which today is run as a co-operative.[12] A further prophecy foretold that: 'The day will come when fire and water shall run in streams through all the streets and lanes of Inverness.'[13] This grisly prophecy was fulfilled when gas and water pipes were laid throughout the town.

Coinnech died when he was called in by Lady Isabella Seaforth to divine the whereabouts and well-being of her husband Kenneth. Initially Coinnech refused to give many details saying only that he was well and in France. When pressed by the lady, he gave a true account that Lord Seaforth was currently forgetful of his family and 'was on his knees to a fair lady, his lips pressed to her hand'.[14] Lady Seaforth ordered the Seer to be executed instantly by being placed head-first into a burning tar-barrel filled with sharp spikes – the death of a witch.

As he was about to be killed, the Seer prophesied the end of the Seaforth family. He said that the last of the line would be deaf and dumb, and would be the father of four sons whom he would follow to the tomb. The house would be inherited by a widow from the East and, as a sign that this prophecy was about to fulfilled, the four great neighbours of the Seaforths – the

Gairlochs, Chisholms, Grants and Raasays – one each would be buck-toothed, hare-lipped, half-witted and a stammerer.[15] The fulfilment of that prophecy is said to have come about at the beginning of the 19th century. But the Brahan Seer's salutary fate shows the cost of a seer speaking the truth.

A female seer, *Bantighearnea Lathuir* or The Lady of Lawers, lived on the shores of Loch Tay in Perthshire sometime in the 17th century. She was an Appin Stewart, from Argyll, possibly the wife of a younger brother of Sir James Campbell, the sixth laird of Lawers. Her prophecies relate to the local area of Breadalbane and were written in a book, called the Red Book of Balloch, 'shaped like a barrel and secured with twelve clasps in the charter room of Taymouth Castle'.[16] She made many prophecies concerning the tree that she planted next to the now ruined church of Lawers, using the growth of the tree as a marker for future events. When the tree reached the height of the gables of the church, the Church of Scotland would be divided, an event that took place when the congregation left the Church of Scotland and joined the Free Church in 1843. When the tree was the same height as the ridge on the house of Balloch, then Taymouth would be without an heir, which took place in 1862 when the second Marquis died. The Lady foretold that whoever should cut down her tree would come to an bad end. When John Campbell and his neighbour laid an axe to the tree in 1895, everyone remembered the prophecy. Campbell was gored to death by his own Highland bull, while his assistant lost his reason, and had to be removed to the district asylum.

She also foresaw the Highland Clearances, 'The sheep's skull will make the plough useless', an event she said would take place in the time of 'John of the three Johns, the worst John that ever was'.[17] Tayside saw its own share of tenants forcibly cleared off the land to make way for sheep during the early years of the second Marquis. Her prophecy that 'a time will come when Ben Lawers will become so cold that it will chill and waste the land around for seven miles', sounds like a glacial ice age yet to come, and is a prophecy still outstanding.[18]

Healing is sometimes part of the seer's array, as documented by the Reverend Robert Kirk:

> The Charmer will Extract a Mote out of a persons Eye at many miles distant, only they must first, (Spaniel-like) see and smel ate something worn by the patient … [He] fills his mouth with water, laying his hands on it; when he has muttered the spel to himself, he powrs the water out of his mouth into a very clean vessel, and lets see that very mote in it.[19]

This very skill was possessed by Biddy Cosgary, who lived in the village of Killeaden, Co Mayo, in about 1902. She performed miracle cures for eye ailments, often at a distance. Her method, on being approached for help, was to take a cup and saucer to a nearby well and fill the cup. Returning, she made the client sit opposite and look at her as well as he could. Taking a sip of the water, she would roll it around her mouth and mumble invocations, then bend forward, spit the water from her mouth into the saucer, and the offending obstruction appeared floating in the liquid. She never touched her clients. Her reputation was considerable and two beneficiaries of her treatment maintained that the eye obstruction vanished as Biddy spat out the water into the saucer. This process is similar to many shamanic extraction methods worldwide. Biddy's cure could only be performed on Mondays or Thursdays, and might only be attempted nine times in total for any individual. She was reluctant to speak about the spirit who helped her, merely referring to her as 'the Saint of the Eye':

> My charrum is given from a man to a woman and from a woman to a man. 'Tis only praying to the Blessed Virgin and the Saint of the Eye. Sure, yis, there is a Saint of the Eye up in heaven. Well, when anyone come to me, a good neighbour or a well wisher, and ask me would I cure the eye for thim, thin I should bring a drop of spring water from the well and to take it in my mouth and to kape me mouth closed and say those prayers and worruds to the Blessed Virgin and the Saint of the Eye. Then, savin your presence, I let the water down out of me mouth into a white plate and you'll see in that water whatever injury is in the eye. And to do that three times. It mightn't come

> the first time … There did a letter come over out of
> England to me and told me that a young boy I knew …
> got something in to his eye that hurted it, and the eye
> was keeping bad. Well, I tuck and done the charrum
> for him. And the first drop of water I let down out of
> me mouth what was in it but a big piece of grass.[20]

The boy wrote, stating the hour and day of his relief, which was simultaneous with Biddy's long-distance extraction.

Healing charms and blessings to relieve sickness remain at the heart of Irish culture; they are specific to certain ailments or conditions and usually run in families, jealously guarded and passed on to willing inheritors, but they are rarely given out to the uninitiated. Some ageing charm-keepers find it hard to pass on their power because so few are willing to take up the service and responsibility that accompany this knowledge. Such charmers are in demand, day and night, being called out to attend the injured regardless of the time. The use of charms goes completely undocumented, although everyone in an Irish community knows who to go to in need. Nor is this service something of the past. For example, a woman with the charm for staunching blood was called to the Royal Infirmary, Belfast, after a terrorist explosion injured many bystanders during the recent troubles. She was called in to halt blood-loss before emergency medics could even start triage, and many people owe their lives to her.[21]

Charms are not merely about word formulas. The manner of transmitting a charm involved the passing of the power to perform the healing also. Some healing skills were believed to be passed more successfully to a child before its baptism, and even before it could speak or understand. Long-distance healing or diagnosis is often accompanied with the seer receiving the physical symptoms that echo those of the sufferer. The sense of seeing through the eyes of others, or experiencing their emotions, is also common. An Irish seer and healer of my acquaintance, frequently picks up the symptoms of someone who is about to visit or call her in this way. She may experience the pains of a toothache which is not hers, for example, and shortly following, the one needing relief will phone her. Because she has the second sight also, by her foreknowledge she will know the nature of the person and their illness already.

The seer, Eilidh Watt, a native of Skye, has written of her own experience of the second sight. Apart from seeing the doubles of people distant or dead, and the usual troublesome apparitions that seers endure, she often finds herself to be the answer to someone's need or prayer, as when she attended a public meeting and found herself sitting next to two nuns. During the interval, they turned and asked her how to teach drama to infants – a subject she knew nothing about. Drawing upon unknown knowledge, she proceeded to give a good account of such a method, and the nuns felt they had been directed to come to the meeting to have their prayers answered. Mrs Watt frequently finds herself having to go out of her way in order to be of service to someone she barely knows, at the command of her seership.[23]

From the ancient world until our own time, the living art and service of seership is both a blessing and a burden. Let us learn more of what is involved.

Calling upon the Ancestors

Ancestors include *all* your forebears, everyone and every being from the sky above to the earth below. They are not far from you, if you call upon them. At least one in your lineage has been blessed with seership or has gained the gift of vision from the eternal *gléfiosa*. Before you step upon this path, it is good to confer with experts who have prior knowledge and personal experience. Stand at a threshold place, between night and day, and call upon one of the ancestral visionaries. Introduce yourself; state that you want to learn from the *gléfiosa*, that you seek a mentor from the ancestors. Still your body, mind and emotions; be attentive in your soul. Note what arises for about 20 minutes. Thank those who showed themselves to you. State that you will return again soon with a question. Record your findings and watch your dreams. Be aware of the substrata of your conscious life; stop and attend when you sense a nearness or a small understanding, when you are tuning into your mentor. At your next session, ask to be shown the responsibilities and services of vision and seership. One ancestral seer, or more, may come to you; with respectful attention, note what they are showing you. This is the beginning that never ends.

CHAPTER 2

Seeing the Invisible

*The vision makes such a lively impression upon
the seers that they neither see nor think of
anything else, except the vision, as long
as it continues.*

Martin Martin, *A Description of the
Western Isles of Scotland*

Through the Gap

The Ballachulish figure, dated 730–520 BC, was found during peat-cutting in an Invernesshire bog in Scotland, and is a thin, long-headed, female figure, shaped from oak. It was discovered underneath a wicker hurdle, interred in the peat, and treated not unlike the many bog bodies that have been found all over Europe from this period. Whatever its original purpose, the figure was disposed of so that it would enter oblivion, let slide into the ancestral realms as an offering. The most eerie aspects of this figure, now in the National Museum of Scotland, are its quartz eyes, which still gaze unceasingly. The right eye is larger than the left, which has an inward turn to it. We could be looking at a seer entranced. The unchanging stare of the seer is distinctive, as related by the Gaelic-speaking Martin Martin, who made a study of seership in his *A Description of the Western Isles*, written in 1703:

> At the sight of a vision, the eye-lids of the person are erected, and the eyes continue staring until the object vanishes. This is obvious to others who are by, when the persons happen to see a vision, and occurred more than once to my own observation, and to others that were with me.[1]

One of the chief features of seership is the making of an aperture with the inner eyes, to look through the gap between this world and the other. In the West Highland divination method, the *Augury of Brighid*, the practitioner makes a tube of their palms, like a telescope, to lengthen this aperture into a tunnel of vision. Looking down into the darkness towards a source of vision, the seer was able to speak what was seen (p.180). The use of hand, mouth and eye is something we will see again and again when discussing methods of seership, for the gap that we look through opens into a totality of seeing that reveals all.

Ways of Seeing

The way in which we perceive meaning has changed considerably since our ancestors' time. Imagine a life without the constant hum of electrical current running through the land; without aircraft scoring the skies with vapour trails; a time without the fumes of cars or the knowledge of labour-saving devices; a time where everything is prepared by hand at a slow pace; when to travel from your home to another place means walking or a horseback ride. Your world shrinks back to a smaller compass where the passing of strangers through your land is a great event, but you don't worry about the world news every night because you don't hear any until several months after the event in question has passed – brought to you at the pace of a walker or rider.

The constant markers of your life are the movements of the stars and moon at night, the circuit of the sun by day, the seasons' round, migrations of animals, the cycles of birth and death, and the daily visitations of the weather. People do not seek solitude naturally, but rather gather together for safety, comfort and mutual support.

You live in a world that is not yet bounded by the kind of assumed knowledge that breeds superiority. The circle of your life is part of a much wider round whose inhabitants are unseen, whose motivations are unclear. Humans are not the only beings in your world alongside the domestic beasts that give you food, drink and clothing. There are wild animals whose movements have meaning to those with the eyes to see. In the bark of the rowan tree, there are faces watching. By the hazel-rimmed stream, the people of peace make their dancing. Up in the high pastures, among the lichened rocks, there are older spirits abroad. The skies themselves are full of haloes of light, speaking of beings larger yet.

While the priest or minister tells you that God is above all, and the scriptures are all the knowledge you need for salvation, you know that there are older beliefs written upon the wind and in the mirrored waters. These unknown matters keep you humble. You give respect to any who can hear what the wind sings, or what the omens of animals might portend. When you stand upon the hillside guarding sheep from the wolves, you sometimes hear a singing from the earth, and you make a blessing that guards your very soul from the call of those who live in the hollow hills, without light of sun or moon to hallow them. You know there are those who have strayed out of the paths of men into the halls of faery, and who never returned home, save only after hundreds of years were past.

You know the common signs and abide by them, because your ancestors told you to respect what is unseen by the signs of its coming. The lamb that you just helped to birth has little chance of life, you know it in your veins by the way it made no struggle to stand up. The red-haired girl who smiled at you in the market and crossed your path has made you feel unlucky, and you should have turned back and not tried to sell your cheeses that day. Didn't the raven itself sit over the roof of the barn and scold for the length of time it took to draw water from the well? You just hope that no-one except the lamb is going to die.

Yes, this is a different world from the one in which we live today. Our modern perceptions are less honed and sensitive. Years of peering at the distortions that come through television, computer and phone screens have detuned our perception of reality and muted our instincts. We can seldom hear or sense what is happening around us because we are too busy, rushing on to the next activity.

The ability to discern an omen is based upon a certain stillness, where perception can dart between what is seen and what is not seen, between serial time and timelessness. There are also those who have the second sight – a gift you are glad you do not possess – for who would want to have the knowledge of death before it strikes, or see the shades of the departed?

Prophets there are also, who have a certain knowing of the shape of things to come, whose words are mysteries to those who hear them, and a miraculous foreknowledge to those who live after they are dead. They see with the unchanging eye and speak with the stern voice of the mountains.

Acquiring the Second Sight

The seer knows neither the object, time, nor place of a vision, before it appears, and the same object is often seen by different persons, living at a considerable distance from one another … If the object is seen early in a morning … it will be accomplished in a few hours afterwards. If at noon, it will be accomplished that very day. If in the evening, perhaps that night; if after candles be lighted, it will be accomplished that night; the later always in accomplishment, by weeks, month, and sometimes years, according to the time of night the vision is seen.[2]

This description of the spontaneity of the second sight is reported by Martin Martin in his 17th-century *A Description of the Western Isles*. Samuel Johnson, who made a visit to the Hebrides in 1773, describes it with his dictionary-maker's rationalism as 'an impression made either by the mind upon the eye, or by the eye upon the mind, by which things distant or future are perceived, and seen as if they were present'.[3]

The 'two seeings' (p.x) bestows a simultaneous vision of what is apparent and what is not normally visible. Where you or I might just see a chair, a seer may see not only the physical chair, but also the spirit of the last person who sat in it who has died, or someone who will die soon, as this story from Martin Martin relates:

My Lord Viscount Tarbat, one of her Majesty's Secretaries of State in Scotland, travelling in the shire of Ross, in the north of Scotland, came into a house, and sat down in an armed chair. One of his retinue, who had the faculty of seeing the second-sight, spoke to some of my Lord's company, desiring them to persuade him to leave the house, for, said he, there is a great misfortune will attend somebody in it, and that within a few hours. This was told my Lord, but he did not regard it. The seer did soon after renew his entreaty with much eagerness, begging that my Lord might remove out of that unhappy chair, but had no other answer than to be exposed for a fool. Some hours after my Lord removed, and pursued his journey; but was not gone many hours when a trooper riding upon the ice, near the house whence my Lord removed, fell and broke his thigh, and being afterwards brought into that house, was laid in the armed chair, where his wound was dressed, which accomplished the vision. I heard this instance from several hands, and had it since confirmed by my Lord himself.[4]

It is well known that the second sight runs through families and is connected with the gene for red hair. But for those who are not so blessed, the second sight can be temporarily acquired by different means, most often by physical contact with a seer. Reverend Robert Kirk gives a method for transmission of seership, suggesting that the operator:

Gird a tether of hair which has bound a corpse to the bier about his middle, then bow his head downward and look back through his legs until he espies a funeral advancing.[5]

This rather grisly method equates the getting of the second sight to contact with the dead. An alternative to this method is to 'peer through a hole [in a tree] from which a knot of fir has been taken'. But if the wind changes while the operator looks through the knot-hole of a piece of wood – as parents frequently mock-warn their grimacing children – he is in danger of his life. This purposeful looking through a hole makes a portal or aperture from our everyday world into the other. We will discover more of this method when we look at the *frith* (p.176).

The temporary ability to see what the seer can perceive is often conveyed by standing where the seer is, as we see here from Martin Martin's description:

> A man and his brother were travelling to the cave at Kilpatrick in Arran which was used as a church during the times of persecution. The man stopped suddenly as they approached the cave, pointing to the rocks on the shore, exclaiming, 'Do you see that?' His brother could see nothing. 'Place you foot on mine and look again,' said the man. As soon as he had done so, the brother saw his kinsman's wraith at the spot. It was the very place where later he met his death.[6]

Sometimes the way to gain the second sight is to place one's foot under the right foot of a wise seer, who will place a hand upon one's head. Looking back over the seer's right shoulder, one may behold, 'a Multitude of Wights, like furious hardie men, flocking at him hastily from all quarters, as thick as Atoms on the Air'.[7]

This flocking of atoms, or press of 'hardie men', about the seer might be an early description of the spirits of the air, or the widespread phenomena of orbs, which many people have recorded with photographs on a digital camera. When amplified, these orbs appear like flower heads. It is clear that such phenomena have always been around us, but our inability to see or photograph them until now has prevented us from being aware of 'atoms on the air'.

Sometimes the invitation to see with two eyes at once has a more intimate connotation, as in the 15th-century legend of the prophetic seer, Thomas of Ercledoune, where he is invited to lay his head in the lap of the faery queen, who shows him the ways that lead to the otherworld:

> Thomas, soothely, I thee *hight* [call],
> Come lygge [lie] thyne hede downe on my knee,
> And [thou] sall se the fayreste sight,
> That ever sawe mane [man] of they contree.[8]

Orkney healer, Elspeth Reoch, reported in 1633, that her faery ally told her to take an egg and roast it, to gather the sweat of the egg for three Sundays in a row and then, with unwashed hands, to wash her eyes with the egg's sweat and she would then be able to see and know anything she desired.[9] In Wales, 'descendants of a person who has eaten of the eagle's flesh shall be possessed of second sight to the ninth generation'.[10]

The one who opened up more discussion on the second sight than at any other time in history was the Reverend Robert Kirk, the Episcopalian minister of Aberfoyle who had served in the parish of Balquidder for over 20 years. He was a Gaelic speaker, who collected faery lore and information on the second sight from his parishioners, which he published in his book *The Secret Commonwealth* in 1690. But first he prepared a Gaelic Bible that was financially underwritten by Robert Boyle, now considered to be the father of modern chemistry. Kirk's research was of great interest to many antiquarians of the late 17th century, including members of the Royal Society and Samuel Pepys, spy master for King Charles II. Pepys' own interest in second sight was a professional one. He had already investigated Spanish seers who were reported to be able to see things remotely.[11] The appropriation of seership by governments was not confined to the 17th century, for 'remote viewing' by seers was to became a preoccupation of both the Soviet state and the USA, who wished to utilize the skill for defence purposes in the 20th century.

Seership and Vision

The two-headed statue on Boa Island stares over Loch Erne in Co. Fermanagh, with wide, almond-shaped eyes, looking in two directions at once, like any seer. What happens when seers have a vision? What is it they are seeing and how? To answer this, we have to enter into a holistic view of the universe, where the side of reality perceived with our senses is fused with its other, unseen side. These two sides create one fabric. Most people perceive just the everyday reality around with their five senses and are impervious to the other side of reality, but there are exceptions that everyone has experienced. Parents can be aware of their children's danger, even at distance. We are able to 'pick up' when someone is about to phone us, largely because the caller has been thinking about us. Animals 'see' things that we don't perceive, as when a horse refuses to go over a dangerous bridge. Such instinctive experiences are about perceiving the whole of reality, not just its apparent side.

All seership and vision is a means of perception and observation by the extrasensory senses. The old Irish word *taidbsiu* – meaning a spectre, apparition or vision of the second sight – also has the root meanings of 'appearance' or 'observation'.

Seers envision both sides of reality simultaneously, as if time and space had contracted to that single moment, just as a radar device can detect the presence of aircraft or shipping far distant. Actions past, or yet to come, reveal themselves in the present moment. Those whose seership is trained can look, when questioned, at a particular issue and answer by a kind of echolocation; the question focuses the vision and enables the search through time and space. Some seers enhance their signal through the guidance of spirit-allies, who may include ancestors, or spirits who have never been incarnate, the commonest being faeries or other beings whose otherworldly perspective enables answers to be found.

Some seers experience the overshadowing of a mood or emotion that is not their own: a sudden changing of temperature, a narrowing of focus, a sharpening of definition through the medium of their senses. In the Irish story of Cormac mac Art's excursion into the otherworld, he sees:

> a bright well within the enclosure with five streams
> flowing out of it. Hosts of people were coming to take

turns and drink from its waters. Above the well grew everlasting hazel trees. The purple hazelnuts dropped into the well and the five salmon that were in the well cracked them open and sent the husks down the streams. The sound of the streams falling was sweeter than any music made by men. The well that you saw with five streams is the Well of Knowledge, and the streams accord to the five senses by which knowledge is discerned. No-one can gain knowledge who has not drunken a draught from the well and the five streams. The people of the gift (*aos dana*) are those who drink of both.[12]

These streams of the senses also flow in us. They have two inter-connected dimensions that enable the seer to perceive with more vision. The physical senses provide our day-time or ordinary world understanding, but our subtle senses come into play to reveal to us the night-time or otherworldly understanding. The British poet, Taliesin, speaks of seven senses in his 'Song of the Macrocosm':

> I praise the one who did bestow
>   my seven senses,
> from fire and earth, water and air:
> the mist and flowers, the wind and trees,
> and much skilful wisdom …
> One is for instinct, two is for feeling,
>   three is for speaking,

four is for tasting, five is for
  seeing, six is for hearing,
seven is for smelling.[13]

Most often, we are too busy or preoccupied to fuse both dimensions of our senses into one array. Using both sensual dimensions at once, is like a pair of imaging scanners working simultaneously from outside and inside a subject. Not everyone is arrayed the same. Those with visual acuity in the ordinary world may not have it when it comes to seership work: artists, for example, may discover that their more developed inner sense might be touch, rather than vision. Martin Martin speaks of the seership that arises through sound or smell:

These spirits used also to form sounds in the air, resembling those of a harp, pipe, crowing of a cock, and of the grinding of querns: and sometimes they have heard voices in the air by night, singing Irish songs; the words of which songs some of my acquaintance still retain. One of them resembled the voice of a woman who had died some time before, and the song related to her state in the other world. These accounts I had from persons of as great integrity as any are in the world. Things also are foretold by smelling, sometimes as follows. Fish or flesh is frequently smelled in a fire, when at the same time neither of the two are in the house, or in any probability like to be had in it for some weeks or months; for they seldom eat flesh, and though the sea be near them, yet they catch fish but seldom in the winter and spring. This smell several persons have, who are not endued with the second-sight, and it is always accomplished soon after.[14]

Very few personal accounts of seership by actual seers have ever been published, and even fewer sources speak of the consequences of having this gift. The reasons for this disparity may be summarized easily. Most innate seers do not regard their gift as an advantage, occuring as it does without their volition and at inconvenient times. The implications of the truth arising from the sight are difficult to live with. The Cassandra syndrome, by which the reports of seers are frequently disbelieved, is another factor that keeps seers silent. The consequence of reporting the vision sets seers apart from their fellows. It is only within the modern era that people have sought to learn these skills with any great desire; whereas, in earlier centuries, many seers sought to lose the gift by whatever means possible, so difficult was its possession.

Inward Vision and the Door Without a Key

> It is one of the tenets (among the Faeries) that nothing
> dies, but (like the sun and moon) everything goes in a
> circle, lesser or greater, and is renewed and refreshed
> in its revolutions. Also, that every body in the creation
> moves and that every living being has another animal
> moving on it, and so on, to the smaller atom that is
> capable of being a receptacle of life.[15]

This extract from Kirk's *The Secret Commonwealth* reveals an important insight into the nature of life, and also into the ways that seers and visionaries work. Just as fractals in chaos physics reveal an orderly repetition of the essential design of matter at all levels of life, so the whole universe is part of an enfolded pattern. Wherever we go, this pattern is present, whether we focus our attention or not. This pattern is what seers access when they work, but it requires a deeply focused attention to observe it. Just as a skilful smith forges a blade by bending and turning the metal over and over, until the blade takes on a concentrated folding and refolding pattern that is beautiful to behold, so seers and visionaries must enter deeply the enfolding of the universal pattern.

One of the secrets of poetic seership is the inwardness vision. This is a method whereby the poet steps ever deeper into the vision by following this patterning further inward. The kind of telescopic vision that results from this is already known to us from childhood, when we used to recite rhymes and songs that practise inwardness. We see it demonstrated in the traditional song, *The Green Grass Grew All Around* where each verse of the song goes deeper, revealing a smaller and smaller thing, while the chorus repeats all these nesting images as a list in which the singer is returned to the world of normal perspective again.

> Oh, the feather on the bird, and the bird
>   in the nest, and the nest on the leaf,
>
> And the leaf on the twig, and the twig on the
>   bough, and the bough on the branch,
>
> And the branch on the limb, and the limb
>   on the tree, and the tree in a hole
>
> And the hole in the ground, and the green
>   grass grew all around, all around
>
> And the green grass grew all around.[16]

An example of this kind of vision is revealed in the *Lebor Gabala Erenn*, the Book of the Irish Invasions, where the Milesian poet Amairgin invokes the land of Ireland in a series of poems. Finally, he is called upon to abate the wind that keeps blowing the Milesian invaders away from its shores. He brings them closer to shore with the help of this invocation, sequentially spiralling nearer to the spiritual nature of the island:

> I seek the land of Ireland.
> Forceful is the fruitful sea,
> Fruitful the serried mountains,

Serried the showery woods,

Showery the cascade of rivers,

Cascaded the tributaries of lakes,

Tributaried the well of hills,

Welling the people of gatherings,

Gathering of Tara's king,

Tara, hill of tribes,

Tribes of Míl's people,

Míl's ships and galleys,

Galleys of mighty Eire,

Eire, mighty and green.

A crafty incantation,

Craftiness of Bres's wives,

Bres, of Buaigne's wives,

Great Lady Eire: Eremón harried her,

Ir and Eber sought for her –

I seek the land of Ireland.[17]

Immediately on hearing this invocation, the wind calms itself and the Milesians begin to disembark on the southwestern coast. This poem is the nature of a magic spell where Amairgin uses his poetic vision to go deeply into the heart of Ireland and to envision Milesians as *already being* kings at its innermost, sacred province at Tara. By aligning himself with the sacred patterning of Ireland, he even includes himself among those who have previously sought out Ireland in order to be its overlords. This inward vision is an intrinsic part of the prophetic skill of *teinm laegda*, by which vision poets circle nearer to the source of their enquiries (*see* p.97).

Dream Divination

The openings and gaps through which the soul passes between the worlds are the very ways that modern culture ignores: dream, vision and meditation. While many are keen to enjoy the kicks of vision through recreational dance or drugs, few notice the nightly portal through which we all pass: the dream that lies behind the 'door without a key'. Dream is the portal of seership that we all share. Dreams give foreknowledge and can be prophetic, but they always reveal the underside of life's topside.

Dream divination is probably one of the oldest kinds of seeing. Throughout the ages there are common dream themes with stipulated meanings, as we see from a small tract on divination housed in Trinity College, Dublin, part of which deals with dreams. The entries and their associative interpretations are terse, but they do give a flavour of the kind of associations that certain dream themes suggested.

A dead King denotes shortness of life. A King dying denotes loss. A King captured alive denotes evil. A brilliant sun denotes blood. A dark sun denotes danger. Two suns in one night, disgrace. The sun and moon in the same course, battles. To cut the nails denotes tribulation. A gold girdle around you denotes envy. To sow tares denotes combats. To catch birds by night denotes spoils by day. Birds flying from you by night denotes the banishment of your enemies. To carry arms denotes honour.[18]

In our time, when psychological forms of interpretation have become common, it is necessary to remember that the poet and the seer lived by the interpretation of metaphor and vision that arose from otherworldly encounters, and they had their own expertise.

But, some dreams were difficult to interpret and they needed the assistance of one who lived and moved in the world of metaphor. The Welsh chief poet, Taliesin, travelled into Brittany and interpreted the dream of King Iud-hael, who dreamed that he saw himself seated on a throne at the top of a steep mountain; before him was a huge pillar stretching from earth to heaven, illuminated by many candles. On the pillar hung weapons, armour, vestments and gospel books. Beside him was girl called Pritell, daughter of Ausoc, whom he had seen the previous day and desired. She told him that this pillar should be given to him; and then Iud-Hael awoke. Taliesin revealed that through Pritell, Iud-hael would have a son who would be a great king at the beginning of his career, and end it as a cleric.[19]

In the *Féilire Oengusso*, an early Irish calendar of saints' days, we hear of the dream of Baíthine, one of the companions of Columcille, in which he saw three chairs in heaven: a throne of gold, one of silver and another of glass. Columcille's interpretation of the dream was that the throne of gold belonged to Ciarán, the carpenter's son, for his honour and hospitality; the throne of silver belonged to Baíthine for his purity and clarity of faith; and the throne of glass belonged to Columcille himself, for the beauty and frailty of his own faith.[20]

After the age of poets and saints, such community dreaming fell to others. A traditional Scottish ritual for locating missing people involved purposeful dreaming. If a ship did not return home, a virgin woman of strong mind was asked to sleep and send out her spirit to seek for its whereabouts. But, if the wind should change while she was asleep and out of her body about her task, she was thought to be in danger of losing her way home, hence the need for a strong-minded woman! Her dream report on waking would send rescuers to discover the wreck or any survivors.[21]

Dream is a sure way of seeing through the fabric where our world meshes with the other. It enables the invisible to become visible, even though we may not yet aspire to the second sight.

Dreamscapes

What arises in the landscape of dream is the illumination of the otherworld, sending a light into your everyday awareness. When you awake, be still, keep consciousness soft and unfocused, so that you retain the dreamscape; don't immediately think about the day's plans. What do you feel or sense on awakening? What are the chief themes, metaphors, images, landscapes that you dreamed? Is there anything that could be about events past, present or to come? What connects most strongly? What does it evoke in you? What intrigues, frightens or excites you? What do you know, deep in your soul, from this dream? By what title could you call this dream? What is the dialogue that begins between you and the otherworld through the message of this dream? Feel the metaphor beyond the literal. Keep away from dream encyclopedias that purport to interpret; use the symbolism of your own awareness, not someone else's. Don't psychoanalyse or chase away your experience. Keep faith with your dream; in the days that follow, draw it, walk it again, interview those whom you met there. Be alert for the resonances of the dialogue. Take your dream into meditation or revisit its landscapes. What is the gift you are given? What is the task for you to perform? What is the story that is living you?

CHAPTER 3

Faery Seership and the Otherworld

Gin [If] ye ca' me imp or elf,

I rede [advise] ye look weel to yourself;

Gin ye ca' me fairy,

I'll work ye muckle tarrie [much trouble];

Gin guid neibour ye ca' me,

Then guid neibour I will be;

But gin we ca' me seelie wicht
    [blessed wight or being]

I'll be your freend baith day and nicht.

Robert Chambers, *Popular Rhymes of Scotland*

The People of Peace

This advice from the mouth of a faery reminds us that respect is the basis of all relationships. Nowhere in Celtic lore is this more important than in our dealings with the faeries, especially now that so mighty a gulf lies between traditional and 21st-century understandings of faeries. What are now considered to be imaginary dragonfly-winged beings of tiny size, of no account, in traditional lore are considered to be dangerous, capable of inflicting harm or death upon people and livestock. Their haunts were, by common consent, avoided by humans. Few would now be afraid of, or respectful to, any modern faery concocted by human imagination. This is why the true people of peace are called 'faeries' in this book, to distinguish them from the trivialized 'fairies' of modern delusion.

Faeries are traditionally held to be the elder race that inhabited the earth before humankind. They are beings of power and influence, who have the primary governance of the earth, sea and air. They are neither tiny nor insubstantial, and their influence is so powerful that it can be deadly if the contract between humans and faeries is not impeccably upheld. Many Irish stories tell of earthly conflicts that begin as a result of an injury to individual faeries, brought about by human greed or thoughtlessness.

Considerable bodies of faery lore exist throughout Britain and Ireland, relating the nature of faeries, called the *sí* or 'people of peace' in Ireland and *tylwyth teg* or the 'fair folk' in Britain. There is a common belief among the Gaels that faeries are the elder race, and that they came to earth after Lucifer and the fallen angels began the descent to their own realm. When the Creator saw that heaven's doors were open, and that others of the heavenly realm were being sucked out of it, a command was given that those who were out should remain out, and those who were in should remain in. The beings who had been sucked out in Lucifer's wake, found themselves exiled in the middle realm of earth, where they made their home.

The elder faeries of Ireland, the Tuatha de Danaan, are 'the lordly ones of the hollow hills'; rather than being of diminutive size they are somewhat larger than humans. The reported size of faeries has shrunk over centuries of different accounts, for they can be whatever size they wish: that which was thought small is large, that which was thought large becomes small. The further into the otherworld we go, faeries and other beings that we encounter grow larger; the further into our own world we travel, the smaller such beings appear. Whenever we encounter 'little/bigness', it is connected therefore to the seer's inward vision that we explored in Chapter 2. It is also a feature of the greater dead, the ancestors, as St Patrick learns when he and his priests are approached by two Fenian heroes of the ancient time: 'they were seized with fear and horror at the sight of these enormous men, the warriors of an earlier age, together with their great dogs.'[1]

The link between the faeries and the ancestors has always been a close one. It was often thought that those who pass into the realms of the dead became part of the faery realm, a concept that we see in the many Celtic accounts of the greater dead feasting in the hollow hills of the world beneath. Reverend Robert Kirk, whose 17th-century 'anthropological study' of faeries and seership, *The Secret Commonwealth of Elves and Faeries*, confirms that 'several who go to the siths [faery hills] … befor the natural period of their lyf expyr, do frequently appear to them'.[2]

Faeries reside at specific locations, although they may move from one dwelling place to another, in the manner of early hunter-gatherers, as the season changes. Wherever you are on earth, then you stand on some faery clan's turf, and the way you behave there is noted by the faeries. Because of this, the early Celtic attitude to them was one of respect and fear, not of familiarity and disbelief. The site of a building was carefully decided, to regard those whom such disruption might displace. The haunts of faeries were left well alone, and those whose work took them up into the hills to shepherd the beasts during the summertime used precautions of talismans, charms and prayers.

The places between the worlds where humans and faeries might meet are frequently the threshold zones: where water meets land, where mountains rise from valleys, where springs gush out, where two trees make a gateway. All of these are 'doors to faeryland'. Negotiating these threshold zones by walking between worlds in dream, vision or on foot, was the work of seers and visionaries. Sometimes people strayed into faery regions at their peril. This invocation was made by 14th-century Welsh seers when they needed to enter the forest where faery spirits lived:

> To the King of the Kindly Ones
>   and to his Queen:
>
> Gwyn up Nudd, who lives within
>   the forest yonder,
>
> For love of your lady, permit us
>   to enter your dwelling.[3]

Gwyn ap Nudd is the faery king whose spirit is seen in the Neath Valley of South Wales, and who has his dwelling in Glastonbury Tor. He is also a leader of the Wild Hunt, a retributive band of spirits who come to chase those who have broken faith with the faeries, or violated their unseen boundaries.

In keeping with the traditional connections between humans and faeries, Kirk remarked that the conflicts and wars of the human world are often preceded by a war among the *sí*. Gaelic lore abounds with such stories of conflict between the faeries, so that some faery hosts are called 'the seelie (or blessed) court' while their opponents become 'the unseelie court'. The 12th-century Irish *Accalam na Senórach* (The Colloquy of the Ancients) speaks of the war between the *sí* of Ibrecc of Assaroe and Lír of the Sí of Finnachad. Lír sent a bird with an iron beak and a tail of fire to lodge on a window of the Sí of Assaroe, until every weapon in the place fell onto the heads of the people.

It continued hurling missiles for the course of a year until the Fenian hero Caílte stopped it.[4]

The faery requirement for truth and justice is the primal drive in their dealings with humans, which are not without gifts and exchanges.

Gifts and Exchanges

From earliest times, human respect for the faeries was shown by a sense of neighbourliness, as here in Lady Augusta Gregory's account of Old Deruane, a man who lived on the island of Aran, in the west of Ireland, with his faultless sense of hospitality to the faeries:

> This island is as thick as grass with them, or as sand; but good neighbours make good neighbours, and no woman minding a house but should put a couple of the first of the potatoes aside on the dresser, for there's no house but they'll visit it some time or other. Myself, I always brush out my little tent clean of a night before I lie down, and the night I'd do it most would be a rough night. How do we know what poor soul might want to come in? [5]

From antiquity, the faeries were honoured by the custom of making offerings of milk or cream, in this case to a *gruagach* or brownie on the Western Isles of Scotland:

They had an universal custom, of pouring a cow's milk upon a little hill, or big stone, where the spirit called Browny was believed to lodge: this spirit always appeared in the shape of a tall man, having very long brown hair. There was scarce any the least village in which this superstitious custom did not prevail. I inquired the reason of it from several well-meaning women, who, until of late, had practised it; and they told me, that it had been transmitted to them by their ancestors successfully, who believed it was attended with good fortune.[6]

The gifts did not come from humans alone, for the faeries were good givers to those who did them honour. The most famous pipers in all Scotland were the MacCrimmons, whose gift was first bestowed upon Iain Og MacCrimmon; he was playing his pipes when a faery woman came and gave him a silver chanter, along with this prophecy:

> Your beauty and the music of your pipes
> Have won a faery lover to you;
> To you I hand the silver chanter
> To be sweet and faultless under your fingers.[7]

Another source relates that two faery women came across the young MacCrimmon asleep and one blinded him in one eye.

The second banshee, however, gave him the gift of the chanter in order to compensate for this loss.[8] This latter story relates to the tradition of the *corrguineacht* (p.123) and of Boann (p.198), in which one side of the body was believed to be in the otherworld, while the other walked in the apparent world.

Many of the greatest bonds lay between the true faeries and humans seers; not only are faeries 'clearly seen by those men of the Second Sight', but they may also bestow it upon those whom they favour.[9]

The gift of second sight or seership was bestowed on Christian Lewinstoun of East Lothian in 1597, whose divinatory skill derived, she said, from her daughter who 'was tane away with the Farie-folk'. Alison Peiron, from Fifeshire, in 1588 claimed that faeries would come and sit beside her when she lay sick in bed and promised that she would never want if she would be faithful and keep promises.

The keeping of promises and a truthful heart required a great deal of human beings, who are not best known for either ability, but they remain the touchstone of all faery alliances, as we can see from looking at any faery story where the human partner in the contract is required to do, or refrain from doing, an action that will break the contract. Cunning woman, Elspeth Reoch from the Orkneys, swore that she gave up her powers of speech in order to gain the help of her faery spirit's skills.[10]

A curious way of calling upon a man's faery-allies, in order to force them to be an oracle, is given by Martin Martin:

It was an ordinary thing among the over-curious to consult an invisible oracle, concerning the fate of families, and battles, &c. This was performed three different ways; the first was by a company of men, one of whom being detached by lot, was afterwards carried to a river, which was the boundary between two villages; four of the company laid hold on him, and having shut his eyes, they took him by the legs and arms, and then tossing him to and again, struck his hips with force against the bank. One of them cried out, 'What is it you have got here?' Another answers, 'A log of birchwood.' The other cries again, 'Let his invisible friends appear from all quarters, and let them relieve him by giving an answer to our present demands': and in a few minutes after, a number of little creatures came from the sea, who answered the question and disappeared suddenly. The man was then set at liberty, and they all returned home to take their measures according to the prediction of their false prophets, but the poor deluded fools were abused, for the answer was still ambiguous. This was always practised in the night, and may literally be called the works of darkness.[11]

Many bodies of healing and herbal lore are said to derive from the faeries. Rory O'Flaherty, who wrote a description of West

Connaught in 1700, had this to say about Morough O'Lee, a notable Irish healer:

> There is now living Morough O'Lee who imagined he was himself personally in Hy Brasil for two days. By that visit about seven or eight years afterwards, he began to practise surgery and physic though he never studied either in all his lifetime before, as all we that know him since he was a boy can confirm.[12]

Morough had fallen asleep on a fairy fort, and when he awoke he found himself in Tír na nÓg, remaining there for a year studying with the faeries. On returning home he was given a book that contained the cures for all diseases, but was told not to open it for seven years and then he would find all the secrets of healing. His visit had taken three mortal days or one faery year, which is the inverse of what is usual in otherworldly time-slips. Three years after his return, an epidemic swept through the land and many begged him to open the book. As a result of not waiting the full term, he was not able to help them all. Morough O'Lee's book, which is no. 453 in the library of the Royal Irish Academy and known as the *Book of Hy Brasil*, has 93 vellum pages written in Irish during the 15th century. It may have been one of the books of the well-known medical family called Mac an Leagh (Lee), who practised medicine for a least two centuries before the year 1600 in the area of Sligo and north Roscommon.

Another such book was compiled by the physicians of Myddfai in Wales; they were the descendants of the otherworldly Lady of Llyn y Fan Fach, who married a Welsh farmer. Their descendant currently works as a pharmacist in South Wales. The book contains herbal cures commonly practised by country-people, but its transmission is remembered as a faery gift.[13]

Lachlan Macdonald, a crofter from Benbecula, told the story of how the faery queen had been saddened by the lack of wisdom among women, and so she breathed an invitation to all women, by pressing her lips to the stalks of every blade of grass, and every leaf of every plant and tree, to come to her hill. Some scorned the invitation and others deemed themselves wiser than she, but those who answered with their presence, were given a drink from her blue limpet shell containing the essence of wisdom. Those who arrived late lost their share.[14]

But such confident gifts and exchanges between faeries and mortals were about to come under a different scrutiny when King James VI of Scotland wrote in his *Daemonologie* against witchcraft, knowing well that the witches commonly resorted to the faery queen and not, as Reforming ministers believed, to the devil:

> They have ben transported with Phairie to such a hill, which opening, they went in, and there saw a faire Queene, who ... gave them a stone that had sundrie

virtues, which at sundrie times hath ben produced in judgement.[15]

The fruits of such faery friendship were about to be used against those who consulted the faeries and spirits of the local hills and groves.

Spirits Between

Beyond the firmament in which He fixed the shining stars, He placed the ethereal heaven and gave it as a habitation to troops of angels whom the worthy contemplation and marvellous sweetness of God refresh throughout the ages. This also He adorned with stars and the shining sun, laying down the law by which the star should run within fixed limits through the part of heaven entrusted to it. He afterwards placed beneath this the airy heavens, shining with the lunar body, which throughout their high places abound in troops of spirits who sympathize or rejoice with us as things go well or ill. They are accustomed to carry the prayers of men through the air and to beseech God to have mercy on them, and to bring back intimations of God's will, either in dreams or by voice or by other signs, through doing which they become wise.[16]

The beings that ply between earth and heaven, in this extract from Geoffrey of Monmouth's 12th-century *Life of Merlin*, are modelled upon the *daimons* of classical belief. These are the 'spirits between' the divine and human realms, called *daimons* by the ancients, a term that was to be radically remodelled into demons. A report about seership, sent to John Aubrey in the 17th century, relates how the correspondent's father met the seer John MacGrigor and asked him if he might obtain his skill, to which the seer responded:

> He would not advize him nor any man to learn it;
> for had he once learned, he would never be a minute
> of his life but he would see innumerable men and
> women night and day round about him.[17]

To witness such teeming presences forever, was judged to be undesirable and the correspondent's father declined the transfer of the sight.

The work of seership and vision is based upon the seer's fusion of both sides of reality, and also upon the cooperation with the spirits between, who may take different forms. Some flavour of what is involved in this process is conveyed in this extract taken from John Dee's notebook for 1589. Dr Dee was the genius behind Elizabeth I's state mechanism, acting as adviser, astrologer, alchemist and geographer, among other things. I have given it modern punctuation to help clarify the meaning.

There is a body of a body,

And a soule and a Spirite,

With two bodies must be knit.

There be two earthes, as I the[e] tell,

And two waters with the[e] to dwell,

The one is whit, the other red:

The quick, the bodies that be ded.

And one fier in Nature y[s] hidd,

And one ayer [air) which them
    doth y dede, [imbue]

And all it cometh out of one kind.

Mark well man, I they mynde.[18]

It is only by fusion of the two halves of reality that seership and vision are possible. The two earths are the visible and unseen realms; while the two waters of the red and the white, are the two streams of the living and the dead, who come into and out of existence on either side of those two realms. Air is the apparent element in our world while fire is invisible: they both derive from one source. Dee's vision is that of an educated man of natural science and philosophy, and owes some debt to neo-Platonic and other sources, but it is helpful to our consideration of how 'two bodies must be knit' together; for when humans and faeries walk together, a unique alliance is made.

Writing in the late 17th century, Reverend Robert Kirk

speaks of the fusion of the seer with his co-walker, or *co-choisi-che*, literally 'the one who steps with you':

> Some men of that exalted Sight, whether by art or nature have told me that they have seen at these meetings (ordinary funerals, banquets etc. at which faeries may attend) a 'double-man' or the shape of the same man in two places; a Superterranean and Subterraean Inhabitant, perfectly resembling one another in all points, who (the seer) could easily distinguish one from the other ... and so go speak to the man his neighbour, passing by the apparition or resemblance of him.[19]

In Kirk's parlance, a Superterranean is a human being who lives above ground, while faeries are known as Subterraneans, those who live below ground.

Kirk also calls this being 'a reflex-man', or *coimimeadh*, literally a 'co-traveller', who is the part of the soul that may go forth and visit other times and places, which may explain how the image of someone living far distant may also appear in another location.

> [Seers] avouch that every Element and different state of being, has in it animals resembling those of another element ... They have told me they have seen ... a double-man, or the shape of the same man in two

places … They call this Reflex-man a *coimimeadh* or Co-walker, every way like the man, as a twin-brother and companion, haunting him as his shadow and is oft seen and known among men, resembling the original, both before and after the original is dead … If invited and earnestly required, these companions make themselves known and familiar to men, otherwise, being in a different state and element, they neither can nor will easily converse with them.[20]

The *coimimeadh* is the co-walker or ally who accompanies each of us. Kirk further speaks of the co-walker as a being who 'accompanied that person so long and frequently … whether to guard him from the secret assaults of some of its own folks, or only as a sportful Ape to counterfeit all his actions'.[21] Kirk relates that a faery co-walker accompanies every living human, though few are aware of it.

Such invitations to be in conscious companionship with the spirits between, typify the many accounts we have from the witch trials from the late 16th to early 17th century, describing 'first contact' between a human being and a familiar spirit. Combing through the witch trials, in which some of the evidence may have been obtained under torture or duress, is a tricky business but they contain accounts of divining or folk-healing gained from faery allies. The faery–human contract was susceptible to misunderstanding by zealous Reformers and witch-hunters as they made their inquisition of individuals taken up for folk-healing or divination. Whatever faery contract the accused reported, the inquisitors understood it to be 'a pact with the devil'.

Able to perceive the sometimes unspoken desire in the heart of a human being, some faeries make their appearance when the human is alone or in a quiet place. The statement taken from Bessie Dunbar, a poor woman arrested and tried in 1576 for sorcery and witchcraft in Scotland, reveals that she was not in contact with demons, but rather with an ancestor who lived in faeryland. She tells how a very prosaic man called Tom Reid, who said he had died at the Battle of Pinkie in 1547, greeted Bessie when she had just given birth and was grieving for her ailing cow, and worrying about her sick child and husband: 'Sancta Maria, Bessie, why make you such great dole … for any worldly thing?'[22] Bessie told him her worries, and Tom told her truthfully that her child and cow would die, but that her husband would recover. He further instructed her to trust in him, and showed her a vision of the good neighbours (faeries), who lived in the Court of Elfame or Elven Home. Tom also gave her a herb and showed her how to help a beast afflicted by elven enchantment, as well as teaching her many other cures. Bessie made salves and powders to heal many sick people after that.

As an ally spirit, Tom Reid appears to be a very ordinary and neighbourly man, apart from the fact that he was dead and living among the faeries. He comes to Bessie when she is in great need, and serves her at the behest of the faery queen, who is a much more important person in Scottish consciousness than the Devil. Tom's appearances occur largely when Bessie is outside, in nature, and his way of talking reveals him to be a Catholic man, born before the Reformation had reshaped Scotland. But Bessie's accusers were of the Reformed Church and, for them, congress with spirits, ancestors or faeries, not to mention the use of herbal cures or the saying of Catholic prayers to heal, were equally damnable, and Bessie was subsequently convicted and burned.

The idea of the dead inhabiting faeryland was widespread. One of the seers interviewed by Robert Kirk claimed that faeries were 'departed souls attending a while in this inferior state [ordinary world]'.[23] This sense of an ancestral collective, that was the same as or became one with faeries, may well stem from an ancient pre-Christian understanding which, by the 17th century, was beginning to wane in cities and in the rationalizations of the educated, but was still potent among country people who kept the ancient lore.

These ancient ways were pragmatic, gathering to themselves anything that was useful, from whichever level of belief. In this way, we see that another woman accused of witchcraft for her healing skills, Bessie Graham, claimed that she was able to transfer illness onto inanimate objects: 'God teach me to pray to put the ill away, out of the flesh, blood and bone, into the earth and cold stone, and never to come again in God's name.'[24] Sucking or stroking illness away, might also be accompanied by prayer-charms that diminished the sickness. It is clear that such healers didn't see their skills as evil but rather, in the words of Janet Trall's faery familiar, as nearer in teaching to the New Testament: … speak of God, and do good to poor folks.'[25]

In times when people didn't understand the physical causes of illness, they often attributed its coming to the malice and envy of witches, or to malicious faery-darts; the healers and visionaries who dealt with such fears resorted to folk medicine, to faery charms or Christian prayers, opening themselves to accusation. But each of these healers had an ally spirit who instructed them in their healing arts, and who enabled them to detect the connection between physical illness and its spiritual causation and cure. Sometimes these were ancestors, like Orkney cunning woman, Elspeth Reoch, who in 1616 testified that 'a black man came to her … calling himself a faery man who was sometime her kinsman, called John Stewart who was slain by McKay'. Sometimes they were spirits, like the healer Andro Man, who called his familiar 'Christsonday' and whom he supposed to be an angel and God's godson.[26]

The healing of illness was but one task in which familiar spirits could assist. The discovery of lost things by divinatory means was also something that spirits could help with. Bessie Dunlop reported that she could not do this without the aid of her spirit, Tom.

The seer is rarely without some spiritual ally – either faery, animal or ancestor – who informs and verifies, who leads and reveals what is hidden, so that balance and healing can be brought back to our world, making it a better mirror of the otherworld. This same ally comes to invite the seer to enter into the wisdom and see from the perspective of the otherworld, so that he or she gains extraordinary insight that cannot be measured.

Dialogue of Two Worlds

When the time came for the Tuatha de Danaan to retire from the affairs of the world and to enter into the hollow hills as the faery folk, Manannan, the great god of the otherworld arranged how things would be. He assigned a special house to each family and gave three gifts that would protect them: by means of the *Feth-Fiadha*, or 'the invisible protection', no mortal could see them; by means of the Feast of Goibniu, they would escape age and decay; by means of an ever-renewing pig, they would be eternally nourished. Then the Tuatha could be safe within Land of Promise.[27]

This cordon of invisibility about the otherworld typifies our everyday approach to it, which is generally to ignore anything not apparent to our senses. But from the perspective of the seer, the physical and other worlds are not diametrically opposed as our society holds, thinking the visible world alone to be 'the real world'. The dialogue between both shores is forever calling, although many regard steering our lives by that dialogue as fey and chancy. Daring to enter into dialogue with both sides of reality requires courage and faithfulness, certainly.

What we see and what we imagine have one connected life, but it is only when we enter into dialogue with the otherworld that we understand this. Seers and visionaries receive feedback from their ambient surroundings and conditions, though they perceive also what lies beyond the *feth-fiadha*. They know that the spiritual and emotional meaning of life is not found just on one shore of reality, but is brought to us by the tides originating on the further shore, by way of dream, and impressions that we tend to neglect as irrational promptings of no account.

What if we were to live as if that dialogue were the truest thing we ever did? As a hunter examines the grass for the track of the deer, as a lover looks for response in the face of the beloved, so we, too, need to search the hinterland of that further shore with imagination and intelligence.

The dialogue between our world and the other takes place at the thresholds and crossing places of both realms, at notable land features, such as springs, mountains or rivers, or it can happen in dreams, vision and meditation, when the seer attunes the vision of both realms. Dynamic images of that dialogue spring up archetypally wherever we look in the sources, creating matrices of vision, patterns of landscapes that can be entered in spirit, wherein we meet the faery teachers of the seership traditions. As we enter deeply into these patterns and images, they yield their truth.

One such shape is found within the Irish *immram* tradition. *Immram* literally means 'rowing about' and is the word used for the stories of voyages, told in many different periods, that visit otherworldly islands and locations. The earliest *immram* concerns the voyage of Bran mac Febal, who is invited by a faery woman to visit the Land of Women, an island that is inhabited only by women, whom we can recognize as faery women, akin to the Ninefold sisterhood that bestows inspiration and wisdom (*see* p.133). The 8th-century, Irish *Voyage of Maelduin* visits 32 locations. Both 32 and 33 are important numbers that appear throughout Celtic myth, representing the totality of the divine powers.[28] These islands provide a pattern for meditational exploration, for each has a gift to bestow or a wisdom to teach.[29]

The legacy of the *immrama* stories is seen in the Arthurian tradition, where Arthur himself makes a voyage into the underworld of Annwfyn (the In-world) to claim the hero-feasting cauldron of the Lord of Annwfyn in the 9th-century *Preiddeu Annwfyn*.[30] The sevenfold caers or towers of the In-world invite their own visitation.

Visions of the Celtic otherworld abound with paradisal wonders and paradoxes. We encounter again the vision of inwardness, where the small becomes large and the large is reduced to the small, where the juxtaposition of ordinary and extraordinary vision reveal the true reality of seership. The otherworldly tree of the Welsh Perceval text (*Peredur*) is both green and red – one half in leaf, the other half in flame, yet it is never destroyed.[31] The voyaging hero, Maelduin, encounters white sheep who graze on black fields, while black sheep graze on white fields, until the shepherd moves a white sheep onto a white field, whereon it becomes black.[32] King Cormac's four-sided cup of truth is shattered by the telling of three lies, but is restored to wholeness by the utterance of three truths.[33]

All of these motifs are powerful doorways that invite us to explore deeper, so that we enter into the otherworld in truth. With all the power of dream, these images dissolve the *feth-fiadha* that keeps us from seeing the bright vision of the otherworld. But the chief instrument of vision is the branch of the *crann beatha* or 'tree of life'; in the earliest Irish *immram* story of Bran mac Febal, the faery woman shakes it over Bran, causing him divine disquiet until he agrees to visit the land of women.

The silver branch, a branch with bells upon it, that was also a token borne by poets, was a scion of the *crann beatha*, which grew in everlastingness. The shaking of the branch betokened the silence of attention. It was the means of entering the otherworld, a skill known well to the vision poets or *filí* of the Gaelic world.

Thresholds of Meeting – The Co-walker

Visit a site that stimulates ancestral memory in you, from the lore of the place or from your own impressions. Every place on earth has its spirit. Give and offer peace to all directions, and mean it. If there is anger or hatred clouding your senses, do not perform this until you regain equilibrium. Speak gently and with clear intent to those people of peace who may live nearby. Dismiss rainbow faeries with flittery wings and vapid expressions from your consciousness! The people of peace are as far from these popular impressions as a wild animal is from a tame one; just as you don't stroke a lion like a cute little cat, so you don't disrespect the faeries. They will not do your selfish bidding, nor are they granters of wishes. Be as a child in all simplicity, without mockery or irony, with a peaceful heart, with a respectful mind, with a true tongue.

Bring a gift that you've made yourself – a biodegradable craft of your hands, a small cake you've made, a drink you've brewed – or make a blessing or song that includes the inhabitants of the place but leaves no trace to harm to any being. Keep your own form. Don't strive to become like a faery – you are a human. Don't invite the peaceful people into your life unless you first understand what this means. Above all, be honourable in your dealings.

As you go about your life, become aware of the one who walks with you, unseen to all. If it is your desire to know them, and before you proceed, be clear that this is not a relationship you can just drop or neglect as the fancy takes you. This is a companion for life who upholds your soul's good. Imagine what are the terms of your co-walking? What contract stands between you? Think upon the close friendships you already have with humans: what keeps you in friendship, what signals betrayal, what changes must you make, what space do you have to open, how would you wish to be held and regarded in any friendship? Such promises cannot easily be cancelled once they are made.

After considering this, in a quiet place free from interruption, make your own invitation to meet your co-walker. The meeting may follow in meditation or dream, or as you go about your life. A sense of accompaniment is more important than 'seeing'. While you are building trust, ask about small things and see what happens. Keep faith with what results as evidence of your friendship.

CHAPTER 4

Vision Poets and the Dark Cell

Who is the sage that is made by teaching, yet his teaching is not from men? A sage by the inspiration of the sun or of the Boyne.

O'Davoreen's Glossary

The Role of the Poets

Whether it be at the poetic competitions of the Welsh *eisteddfod*, the Gaelic Scottish *mod* or the Irish *feis*; in the Gaelic community of Nova Scotia, among the Welsh Patagonians or in the Irish clubs of Boston; poets may have day jobs as postmen, teachers or housewives, but they still have immense respect in their community. Whence did this respect emanate? What does it signify?

Poetry has been at the core of the visionary experience from earliest times, creating the bridge of metaphor between daily life and the experiences that flow out of the otherworld. The Celtic poet was much more than a versifier: he could be the interpreter of dreams, the envisioner of prophecy, the diviner who sought answers and guidance to dark matters that the ordinary intellect could not decode. Reaching into the far recesses of the visionary darkness, the poet sought out answers, poems and divinations.

The power of the poet's word was legendary, for he could make a satire if his fee had been unlawfully withheld, or if his person had been subjected to insult or dishonour. But his prime function was to uphold honour by means of praise, or the recitation of ancestral wisdom.

Even the infant poet, Taliesin, was able to wreak havoc on the dignity of Maelgwn Gwynedd's poetic retinue when they went up to the king to demand their fee; as they passed Taliesin, he played 'blerwm, blerwm' on his lips with a finger. Ignoring this vulgar gesture, they stood before the king to demand their fee, but all that came out of their own mouths was an echo of his childish 'blerwm, blerwm'. Amazed at their behaviour, the king demanded to know if they were drunk, but the bards were forced to admit that it had been the youthful Taliesin who had caused them to act thus.[1]

The poet could also bless, and the telling of certain stories and poems came with their own special blessings, as we can see at the end of the Middle Irish story of *MacConglinne's Vision*, in which a cleric sees the otherworld as a wonderland composed of food and drink. We are told both the blessing and the poet's proper payment for telling the story:

> The married couple to whom it is related on their first night shall not separate without an heir; they shall not be in dearth of food or raiment. The new house, in which it is the first tale told, no corpse shall be taken out of it; it shall not want food or raiment; fire does not burn it. The king to whom it is recited before battle or conflict shall be victorious. On the occasion of bringing out ale, or of feasting a prince, or of taking an inheritance or patrimony, this tale should be recited. The reward of the recital of this story is a white-spotted, red-eared cow, a shirt of new linen, a woollen cloak with its brooch, from a king and queen, from married couples, from stewards, from princes, to him who is able to tell and recite it to them.[2]

A poet could create magical changes in the landscape or in beasts, making both barren; or his words could cause blisters on the face of his enemy. His satires might be no worse than a fierce lampoon, which would gleefully be spread by gossips and so work its eventual result: to hold up anyone who slighted him in a dishonourable and mocking light. By the poet's word, reputations rose or sank.

We cannot easily understand the role of the poet in the spiritual life of the people from a contemporary perspective, for it was much nearer the role of the *sangoma* in South Africa – a shaman, praise singer and healer, who was the living memory of the tribe. We have the accounts of classical writers to tell us of the early role of the poet in Celtic society, and also the medieval transcriptions of early poetic traditions. Speaking of the state of things before the Romanization of Gaul, Strabo wrote that:

> … among all the Gallic peoples, generally speaking, there are three sets of men who are held in exceptional honour: the Bards, the Vates and the Druids. The Bards are singers and poets; the Vates, diviners and natural philosophers; while the Druids, in addition to natural philosophy, study also moral philosophy.[3]

In AD 10, the Gauls still distinguished between bards and the *vates* or seers, and druids still held a place in society. After the Claudian invasion of Britain in AD 43, the druids, being the British intellectual caste who advised rulers, were savagely suppressed; their pivotal role in the organization of local resistance made them a ready target. The bards remained, along with the divinatory caste of the *vates,* until the institution of Christianity in the late 4th century left just the bards. The function of the Pagan *vates* was inherited by the *filí*, the vision-poets of Christian Ireland. The term *vates*, from which we have the word 'vaticination' or 'prophecy', is paralleled in Gaelic by the word *faith*, and in Welsh by the word *ofydd.*

In Ireland, druidism died the death of professional secession as ecclesiastical positions usurped druidic roles. Christianity blunted the spiritual spearhead of druidism, but it could not suppress the bards and the diviners who took two separate routes. The bards, who versified and sang for a living, held a lower status to those poets who retained knowledge of divination. These became known as the *filí*, who were much more than mere bards. Because of their visionary skill and their ability to practise the Three Illuminations, (*see* Chapter 5) their honour price, under the Irish system of legal restitution, was double that of a bard. Bards did not engage in the divinatory auguries of the *filí*.

The training of the poet was a long affair, taking many years. The pinnacle of the last three years was the learning of a body of prophetic and divinatory skills known as the Three Illuminations. These skills remained the legal equivalent to 'pleading benefit of clergy' in Irish law – anyone who could prove the skills of augury had 'poetic privilege' or an immunity that set him apart. A Scottish anecdote relates how a bard from the Isle of Mull, on hearing he was about to be summonsed, walked to Edinburgh and proclaimed publically at Mercat Cross that he was a poet; he then turned round and walked back home again, believing himself to be covered by poetic privilege.[4]

The power of poets was only seen to be a threat to society after Christianity had been adopted in Ireland, when the semi-druidic status of poets was being questioned by clerics. At the Irish Council of Druim Ceatt in 575, St Columcille was called upon to settle the issue of poetic privilege and a proposal was made to limit poetic power. Many nobles were impatient with the poets' demands for support, especially as their retinues were often extensive. Columcille pointed out to King Aedh, who was for their banishment, that 'the praises they will sing for you will be enduring'.[5] Dallan Forgaill, the chief *ollamh* (doctor) of poetry, composed a eulogy in praise of Columcille in grateful response.

As the descendants of those who once remembered every precedent and story, poets used three levels of transmission, tuned according to the nature of the assembly. The external mode dealt with the revealed, the embodied and open aspects of practice, such as a praise song. The internal mode dealt with the hidden, implicit, latent and inner aspects, which often opened up the metaphorical parallels of a poem to the initiated listener. But the mystical mode conveyed the subtle, secret and with-drawn aspects of the *gléfiosa*, only open to those able to receive the revelation for themselves – a skill that couldn't be taught, for the poet's chief preoccupation was *imbas* or inspiration.

The *filí* were still attached to the courts of Irish lords right up to the Elizabethan wars in Ireland. Thomas Smyth, a 16th-century Englishman who saw them at first hand, gave a disgruntled Tudor view of the Irish, showing that little had changed since the synod of Druim Ceatt in 575 when the suppression of the poets had been first mooted, and writing of the *filí*:

> The fillis [sic] have great store of cattle and use all the trades of the others [i.e. the bards], with an addition of prophecies. These are great maintainers of witches and other vile matters, to the great blasphemy of God and to the great impoverishing of the Commonwealth.[6]

What was it that unsettled people about the poets? It was not just their demands for recompense, nor their skill in praise or satire. Was it perhaps the manner in which they practised their art?

The Dark Schools

The chief method of learning the art of vision among the poets was that of darkness. A Celtic day consisted of a *night followed by a day*, and not a day followed by a night. This understanding is shared by other traditions, where the eve of the day begins a festival, such as the Jewish Sabbath or Christian evensong or vespers. Julius Caesar writes that time was measured:

not by the number of days, but of nights; [the Celts] keep birthdays and the beginnings of months and years in such an order that the day follows the night.[7]

The wise darkness comes first, the better for us to discern and respect the promises of the light that will dawn. In this way, human deeds spring from the depth of dreams, quiet contemplation and the wisdom of the night. There is a different kind of consciousness that emerges when we cross the threshold of twilight and enter night's darkness. It was also part of the training of Celtic poets, who were not merely versifiers, but prophets and diviners also.

Gaelic poets were trained in their craft by entering 'the houses of darkness' as students. These small bothies without windows were their 'classroom'; lying on their backs, students of poetry pursued set themes in the darkness all day, emerging at twilight to recite their compositions to their tutors. The 'university term' of poetry tuition ran over the winter from late September, when all the harvesting would be done, until the call of the first cuckoo.

There are many extant poems of lamentation at hearing the cuckoo, suggesting that this learning in darkness was a wonderful experience, and not the sought-after end of a purgatorial term of tuition. This seeking out of darkness didn't have any sinister purpose, but was a wise use of the seasonal opportunity for a longer darkness, in which poetic themes could be followed in the mind's eye of the imagination without any distraction. A student poet would enter the dark cell before sunrise and leave it after sunset, in the darkest quarter of the year, so that the experience would have been one of continual darkness. Irish poets before the 18th century regarded it strange for any poet to compose while walking or riding about outdoors, so ingrained was this tradition of seeking darkness.

The early monastic response to this in Ireland was to 'write out of doors', in order to distance Christian poetry from that of the Pagan method of poetic composition, as we can see in this anonymous early monastic poem from Ireland:

> A hedge of trees surrounds me,
> A blackbird's lay sings to me;
> Above my lined booklet
> The trilling birds chant to me.
>
> In a grey mantle from the tops of bushes
> The cuckoo sings:
> Verily – may the Lord shield me! –
> Well do I write under the greenwood.[8]

However, it is said that St Columcille meditated on the composition of his hymn *Altus Prosator* – a complex alphabetical poem that tracks the biblical history of the world – by remaining for seven years in a black cell, as a penance for his part in the battle of Cúl Dreimne.[9]

The Memoirs of the Marquis of Clanricarde (1722) relates much of what we know about the bardic schools. Clanricarde tells us these schools were open only to the descendants of poets and their families, and only to those that could read and write well and had a strong memory. The place of study was situated in a quiet place, away from occupation, and was:

> a snug, low Hut, and beds in it at convenient Distances, each within a small Apartment without much furniture. ... No Windows to let in the day, nor any Light at all used but that of Candles and these brought in at a proper Season only ... The Professors gave a Subject suitable to the Capacity of each class ... the said Subject having been given over Night, they work'd it apart each by himself upon his own Bed the whole next day in the Dark, till at a certain Hour in the Night, Lights being brought in, they committed it to writing.' [After dressing, each scholar came into a large room and there performed his poem to his masters.]
>
> The reason of laying the Study aforesaid in the Dark was doubtless to avoid the Distraction which Light and variety of Objects represented thereby ... This being prevented, the Faculties of the Soul occupied themselves solely upon the Subject in hand, and the Theme given; so that it was soon brought

to some Perfection according to the Notions of Capacities of the Students. Yet the course was long and tedious … it was six or seven years before a Mastery was conferred.[10]

Martin Martin, in his *A Description of the Western Islands of Scotland*, bears out this method of tuition:

They shut their Doors and Windows for a Day's time, and lie on their backs with Stone upon their Belly, and Plads [plaids] about their Heads, and their eyes being cover'd they pump their Brains for Rhetorical Encomium or Panegyrick; and indeed they furnish such a Stile from this Dark Cell as is understood by very few … The Poet or Bard had a Title to the Bridegroom's upper Garb – that is, the Plad and Bonnet.[11]

Professor James Garden of King's College, Aberdeen, wrote to the diarist John Aubrey in 1692 to inform him about the nature of bards and their more learned counterparts:

The inferior sort are counted amongst the beggars and rhym [sic] wherewith they salute each house is called *Dan nan Ulag*: (the Meal-Rhym). … He that's extraordinarie [sic] sharp of these bards is named fili, i.e. an excellent poet, these frequent onlie the company of persons of qualitie and each of them has some particular person whom he owns his own master.[12]

Garden reports how the *filí* travelled about, or went on circuit, not unlike a judge, with their retinue of supporters. The spontaneity of their compositions was apposite to the company and to their hosts, as well as drawing upon poems held in memory.

An Irish lament for the lost bardic schools describes the experience of one who had undergone this extraordinary method of training:

> The three forges wherein I was
>   wont to find mental delight,
>
> that I cannot visit these forges wears
>   away the armoury of my mind.
>
> The house of memorizing of our gentle lads
>
> – it was a trysting place of
>   youthful companies –
>
> embers red and shining, that was
>   our forge at the first.
>
> The house of reclining for such as
>   we, the university of art,
>
> poetic cell that kept us from beguilement,
>
> this was the great forge of our trained
>   *anruth* [a grade of poet].

The house of the critic of each fine work of art

was the third house of our three forges,

which multiplied the clinging
   tendrils of knowledge,

wherein the very forge of
   science was wont to be.

Three sanctuaries wherein we took rank,

three forges that sustained the
   loving companies of artists,

houses that bound comrades together.[13]

The slow breakdown of the bardic schools was hastened by a number of factors: the restrictions of the British upon the speaking of Gaelic, and the proscriptions upon the largely Catholic Gaels from partaking in honourable occupations under *Na Péindlíthe* (or the Penal Laws), which held Ireland and parts of Gaelic Scotland captive in successive waves of strictures that led to land dispossession, religious persecution and ultimately to migration.

These accounts of the Houses of Darkness have previously been thought to apply only to the Gaelic tradition, but it is possible that we have overlooked a parallel tradition in Britain. *The Book of Taliesin* provides several references to the dark cell. In his poem '*Buarth Beirdd*' or 'Fold of the Bards', Taliesin tells us about himself in poetic context. A *buarth* is a cow-pen, and a *buarth beirdd* is the place where poets enter into competition with each other, as they still do in *eisteddfodau* today. Taliesin describes this place of competition and how competitors might score in the contest: 'The fold of the bards, who knows it not? Fifteen hundred poles are its qualifications.'[14]

He describes himself: 'I am a cell, I am bower, I am a gathering.' In the *Hanes Taliesin*, the poets who attend on the ruler, Maelgwn Gwynedd, are described as *kulveirdd* (hut-poets), which may indicate the apprentice grade of poets who are still learning in their dark cell.

One of the oldest British poems, *Y Gododdin,* which gives the honour roll of British warriors who fell in a notable 6th-century conflict, gives us another clue. In the 'reciter's preface', the poet Aneurin speaks of himself as with:

> My knees outstretched
> In an earthen house,
> With an iron chain
> Around my two knees.[15]

This part of the poem has been previously taken to indicate Aneurin's imprisonment or his being held hostage by the Bernician enemy host that the men of Gododdin (the area around modern Edinburgh) go to fight, but it may stand in a long bardic tradition of the myth of a young man who is 'imprisoned' by his tutors until he has graduated as a full poet.

The dark cell as a mode of training acquired the metaphor of imprisonment because of it stark and demanding nature. Celtic legend abounds in the stories of youths who are imprisoned, but some of these may be initiatory stories relating to the training of young men who are figuratively held 'hostage' during their education. The mythic theme of the Great Prisoner in British lore, whereby many individuals are said to be imprisoned, lost or confined, is almost certainly influenced by the tradition of the dark cell.

One notable feature of the dark cell method is the way in which the student places his plaid or cloak over himself to ensure utter darkness. This method of working is called 'going under the cloak'. We may speculate whether this part of the bardic training was exported with the Irish slaves who were taken to Iceland to serve, and later intermarry with, the Scandinavian settlers there. We have a record of it when, in 1000, the Icelanders had to decide whether or not to adopt Christianity, because of the conflict that threatened to split Iceland apart. At the Althing (Icelandic assembly), Thorgeir Godi, their lawgiver, went under his cloak for a whole day and a night in order to find an answer to this decision, as reported in *Njal's Saga*:

> 'We cannot live in a divided land,' he said. 'There will never be peace unless we have a single law. I ask you all – heathens and Christians alike – to accept

the one law that I am about to proclaim.' All agreed, pledging under oath to abide by his judgement. He then proclaimed, 'Our first principle of law is that all Icelanders shall henceforth be Christian. We shall believe in one God – Father, Son, and Holy Ghost. We shall renounce the worship of idols. We shall no longer expose unwanted children. We shall no longer eat horsemeat. Anyone who does these things openly shall be punished with outlawry, but no punishment will follow if they are done in private.[16]

Thorgeir's seeking out of advice under the cloak of darkness resulted in the whole of Iceland becoming Christian. The lawgiver went home, took his household gods, which he deposited, in very Celtic fashion, into the nearest waterfall nearby. It is impossible to tell how closely related are Thorgeir's cloak and the dark cell method, although it is clear that many Irish customs were transported to Iceland and may have become adopted there. The Irish 'going under the cloak' method may well have been incorporated into the Scandinavian practice of *uitiseta* or sitting-out at night in vigil to obtain answers to difficulties.

What was their experience in the houses of darkness? What did they find there?

Entering Trance: Going Under the Cloak

The dark cell method of teaching reveals a shamanic way of entering visionary states:

> Darkness is sought by those who seek the vision and inspiration from the otherworld, a vision for which the subject must use his inner, not his outer eyes. The shaman's journey into the otherworld, like the poet's search for the source of inspiration, is hindered by intrusive light.[17]

Darkness enables the subject to enter into trance, the state in which most seers operate. For many people, 'trance' implies a deep state bordering on involuntary somnambulism, but here we mean 'a voluntary state of focused concentration in which visionary impressions appear'. Someone in trance is not entirely oblivious of surroundings, but is so inward in their attention that they enter a state with which we are most familiar by experiencing in dream. The origin of the word 'trance', gives us the clue, for it is from the Latin *transire*, meaning to 'pass over'. Trance is a method by which the ordinary side of reality becomes less important or prominent than the other side of reality.

How does trance happen? What factors enable it? What is its purpose? Trance induction can result from a number of methods, including the movements of swaying and dance; the hearing of repetitious sounds, rhythms and songs; engaging in prayer, stillness, breath-control, hypnotism etc. Trance can be of varying duration, depending on the stimulus that supports it. As the trance deepens, the brainwave patterns alter too, passing from the beta frequency of wakeful attention to the alpha frequency of relaxation, and then dipping into either the theta frequency of calm vision or into the delta frequency of deep sleep, or else a tuned and focused communion with the vision. The chief purpose of trance is to allow the subject to experience union with the two sides of reality at once, or to enter into the unseen, otherworldly side of reality.

The dark cell method works in an economic, slow-sustaining way, with the absence of light plunging the subject into a different state of being, yet not into sleep. Martin tells us that sleep was prevented in the dark cell by the physical encumbrance of a stone held upon the belly, so that the recumbent poet was uncomfortable enough to remain awake. We note, too, that the bardic schools worked over the dark months of the years, from September to the calling of the first cuckoo (usually around the third week of March). In addition, the students entered their dark cell at daybreak, emerging at fall of dark. This is taking darkness to its full limit, with the student poet thus living in a continual round of darkness or semi-darkness. It is a form of light associated with faeryland, which has neither sun nor moon, but only the afterglow of both, as witnessed here by the 12th-century Welsh visitor to faeryland, Elidyr:

It was rather dark, because the sun did not shine there.
The days were all overcast, as if by clouds, and the nights
were pitch black, for there was no moon nor stars.[18]

What results after long exposure to darkness is the dawning
of an inner light, the *gléfiosa* itself. But before that stage, there
are others to be undergone. I can speak of these not only from
personal experience, but from teaching the art of vision to many
individual students, all of whom report orally what they are
experiencing during tuition. After more than 20 years, I have
a clear idea of the stages that most people generally encounter.
After an initial disorientation of being in the darkness itself,
which some subjects cannot tolerate, there arise the phosphenes
that are the patterns, shapes and images experienced within
the eye when there is no light source. These symbols turn up
all over the world, from the early drawings by infants to the
representations in prehistoric cave-art. At this stage, subjects
report disappointment at not seeing anything more concrete,
but these are universally the first steps to trance. Some ignore
the phosphenes and continue to describe the depth or quality
of the darkness, mostly because they have ignored or edited
phosphenes out of an expected result.

The tunnel or vortex visions that typify the next stage
of trance are associated with the poetic sense of inwardness
(*see* p.34) wherein the subject senses being inside a tunnelled
pathway, like looking down a telescope the wrong way or going
deeper into the vision. This stage can be accompanied by a

feeling of spiralling or speeding, so compelling that the subject will be sucked deeper into vision. The compulsion or traction is accompanied by a sense of expectancy. This tunnel stage can be triggered by staring upon specific phosphenes within the trance itself, which then join up to create a larger picture, and may possibly explain the presence of many rock-engravings of spirals or concentric rings in prehistoric and traditional imagery. Looking into the many ripples of a pool that is fed by a spring can have similar effect.

As the vision is sustained, so a sense of emergence and clear vision begins. Instead of being inside the darkness, the subject is in an outside place, often at a different time of day or night. A landscape or scene appears. Some subjects are stunned into silence by this vision, while others rush to describe it. Some are so shocked that something has appeared, they spontaneously retreat to one of the earlier stages of trance, rather like a suddenly contracted telescope, only to slowly extend sections of themselves forward again in careful stages. The physical sense of being present in the landscape of vision is intense and focused. At this stage, the depth of vision and steadiness of sustained trance is clear to see: the subject's feet move like those of swimmers, pulsing gently back and forward as if in water, limbs twitch and eyelids flutter, just like sleepers in the REM stage of sleep.

For every single person the experience of trance is different, depending upon their sensual array, cultural filters and, particularly, upon the theme or question chosen for their trance session, for trance is not entered into arbitrarily or without intent, as some think. Anyone contemplating this procedure might wonder what to do, or how to be guided. But the landscapes of vision are inhabited, and so they are not alone: animals, spirits, ancestors, faeries, gods and companions of many kinds come forward to meet the one entranced. These arrive, according to the issue or question in the heart of the subject: they reveal knowledge, show ways through difficulties, reply, teach or guide. As in a dream, things impossible in our world become possible while entranced: swimming underwater, flying in the air, visiting ancestors, dancing with faeries, being healed by dismantling the body and reassembling it, learning knowledge that cannot be known by ordinary means.

Those who enter into the *gléfiosa* do not readily want to return from it. The sense of oneness with the vision, the immersion in the vision, the companionship and lack of division between the subject and those they meet in vision, all make returning to ordinary consciousness disagreeable, for they have experienced the wholeness of the two sides of reality. This return to ordinary consciousness, and a sense of division from the otherworld, is keenly displayed in the account of Bran mac Febal's return to his native shores.

> Then they went until they arrived at a gathering at Srub Brain. The men [on the shore] asked of them who

it was came over the sea. Said Bran: 'I am Bran the son of Febal.' However, the other [men of shore] saith: 'We do not know such a one, though the Voyage of Bran is in our ancient stories.' Then [Bran's companion] Nechtan leaps from them out of the coracle. As soon as he touched the earth of Ireland, forthwith he was a heap of ashes, as though he had been in the earth for many hundred years. Thereupon, to the people of the gathering Bran told all his wanderings from the beginning until that time. And he wrote these quatrains in Ogham, and then bade them farewell. And from that hour his wanderings are not known.[19]

The timeless wanderings of Bran and the entranced visions of the seer and poet may seem vastly different in kind, but the attempt by Bran to return to his native shores after his long time in the otherworld is comparable to anyone trying to 'become ordinary' again after such a trance. Not only is the seer's vision changed forever, but his fellow men do not recognize him as he once was.

Seership is an art that sets its practitioners apart, which is why the *filí*, the vision-poets, underwent so long a training at the end of which came the learning of the Three Illuminations. It is to these skills we now pass.

Dreaming While Awake

When twilight falls, sit in darkness for a half-hour, holding a theme or question in your heart. Allow the metaphors, images, scenes and stories to arise, without pushing them to be there. The lack of visual and other stimuli helps you focus upon your issue. Allow the darkness to be your teacher and your friend. Your mind will wander, but just lead it back like a shepherd to the issue you are exploring. If total darkness is impossible, then use an eye mask, or place a shawl or blanket over your head and eyes, which is a very traditional method of seeing. If you are inclined to sleepiness, then position some heavy object on your lap, such as a stone, which is uncomfortable enough to keep you wakeful. Notice what arises and don't dismiss what seems irrelevant, mind-wandering aside. Note your findings. You may not find this gives instant results because you are learning to perceive by a different route. Continue and repeat. It is traditional to make your findings into a poem or song, but you could also paint, draw or embroider them. You are bringing the *gléfiosa* out of the darkness into manifestation, so ensure that it has an honourable form to enter.

CHAPTER 5

The Three Illuminations

*Though there be no knowledge of true lore
in all of Ireland but that which you have now left
with us, the men of Ireland should be gathered
in one place to obtain it.*

Acallam na Senórach
(The Colloquy of the Ancients)

I n ancient Ireland, in a secret place, Nechtan kept a covered well. Only he himself and his three cup-bearers were permitted to approach it, for if any unauthorized person looked upon it, their eyes would burst. His wife, Boand, boldly uncovered it and looked within. Immediately, three streams of water flowed forth, injuring her foot, hand and eye. As she fled away from the waters, they followed her, creating the course of the Boyne river (*see* p.199). This myth of the Boyne river shows how Boand steals the knowledge that becomes the heritage of poets. Not only is she injured in her eye, the organ in which the soul is believed to reside, but also in her hand and foot, which have different kinds of eyes, for the whorls upon the fingers and toes are believed to be the points where wisdom enters and are called in Irish, *suile méare* and *suile coise*, or 'the eyes of the fingers/toes'.

What has the loss of an eye to do wisdom? We know the myths of losing an eye in return for wisdom, from the Norse story of Odin, who hangs upon the tree to receive knowledge, to the Irish primal god Balor, who loses an eye when he approaches a cauldron of venom so that his blind eye has to be covered thereafter since his gaze blights all it looks upon. The oldest of the animals, the salmon, while it is stuck fast in the ice, loses its eye to the depredations of the Hawk of Assaroe; the human midwife who goes to assist a faery woman in labour puts some of the healing ointment on her eyes and sees more clearly, only to have a passing faery, whom she can clearly see, come and blind her in one eye afterwards.

As we have seen, the art of seeking wisdom in the heart of darkness was the central core of the vision poets, as before them, the druids sought to bring light out of darkness by entering burial mounds and communing with ancestors.[1] One part of us lies in this world, one part of us in the otherworld; the seeing eye knows the everyday world, the unseeing eye remaining alive in the otherworld and sees its wisdom. In Irish folklore, the vein at the back of a poet's head was believed to be where poetry pulsed, an idea associated with "'the dark part" of one's body which the eyes cannot see.'[2]

The skill that typified the kindling of the *gléfiosa*, the bright knowledge, was the prophetic body of knowledge known as 'the Three Illuminations'. It was these prophetic methods of gaining knowledge that elevated a mere poet to a visionary seer. The Three Illuminations were taught in the final module of the poetic curriculum, and their possession was a distinguishing factor of the immunity enjoyed by poets. Right through to the 13th and 14th centuries, if a poet could demonstrate his skill in these visionary arts, he stood above the law, so respected were they.

The 9th-century bishop-king of Cashel, Cormac mac Cuilleannain, gave an account of them in *Cormac's Glossary*, an early dictionary of primal terms. His definitions of the Three Illuminations are not written with the discernment of experience, but rather the literary interest of a cleric recording arcane matters that people are beginning to forget. We also have many accounts of their use in Irish story and myth, which help to extend our understanding.

The Three Illuminations are individually called *Imbas Forosna*, *Teinm Laegda* and *Dichetul do Chennaib*. Let us find out how they worked.

Imbas Forosna

The word *imbas* derives from the Old Irish *imb-fiuss* or *imb-fess*, meaning 'fullness of knowledge', while the word *for-osna* literally means 'great kindling'. The sense of *Imbas Forosna* is thus 'kindling the fullness of knowledge'. Here is how *Cormac's Glossary* defines its practice:

> [*Imbas Forosna*] reveals every good thing that the poet desires to know or to make clear. It is done like this. The poet masticates the meat of a red pig, or of a dog or cat. Then he puts it upon the threshold stone behind the door and makes an incantation over it, offering it to images of gods. Then he calls his spirits to him to help him and, if what he is looking for is not revealed the next day, he makes incantations over his two palms and calls again upon his spirits that his sleeping should not be disturbed. He places his palms over his eyes and so falls into trance. He is invigilated

as that he is not disturbed or interrupted until his searching is completed, which might be a minute or two or three, or as long as he was supposed to be continuing his offering. This is why it is called *imbas*: 'his two palms' *boiss* upon *im* 'him', one palm over the other upon his cheeks.

Patrick forbade this practice and also that of *Teinm Laegda*, saying that anyone who practised them should not merit heaven or earth, since it went against their baptismal vows. He did however allow *Dichetal Do Chennaib* to be used in their poetic craft because it didn't involve making offerings to demons; the revelation comes directly from the tips of the poet's fingers.[3]

Imbas Forosna was a very purposeful seeking-out of spiritual help by means of a trance-like incubatory sleep, and was used for important decision-making and the ritual discernment of kingly candidates. Its Pagan origins are played up in the making of offerings to spirits but the fact that, in Old Irish, the word for 'meat' – *mír*, and the word for finger – *mér* are so close, may suggest a confusion in the writer's mind. Cormac also makes a clerical wordplay on the word *imbas*, which can also mean 'his two palms'. While it is true that putting the palms over one's eyes is a good way to create a temporary darkness necessary for a trance, Cormac has obviously never seen it practised.

The description shares elements with the *tarbh feis* (*see* p.116) in that the seeker is invigilated and that it may involve a night of searching in vision. We also recognize that such an inspired seeking is analogous to a shamanic soul-flight, where spirits impart wisdom, healing or information to the shaman. *Imbas Forosna* requires a longer fulfilment, and has more ritual elements to it than the other forms. Cormac is unclear himself, saying that it can last a matter of minutes but, in the same breath, the practitioner might need to be invigilated because he is in deep sleep! The direct relationship between the practitioner and his spirits is underscored with the offerings. The animals that Cormac instances – the red pig or a cat or a dog – may have been dedicated to the spirits, and then a ritual meal of the flesh eaten on an empty stomach, in order to call upon the animal's abilities: the headlong speed of the pig and its sensitive nose to seek out food; the night-shining glow of the cat's eyes; the swift hunting of the hound. The practitioner recites his invocation over his palms – a form we see repeated in the Augury of Brighid (p.180).

Cormac tells us *Imbas Forosna* and *Teinm Laegda* were outlawed, but he may be showing his own bias and citing St Patrick as an unimpeachable second, since the rest of his descriptions of the methods do clearly stem from the Christian period.[4]

Teinm Laegda

Teinm Laegda literally means 'cracking open or gnawing the pith or the poem'. Poets used this method for discovering unknown matters, just as a dog sucks out the marrow of a bone. This spontaneous, incantatory method of discovery brought poets to the heart of the matter. The literal chewing of its title is clearly seen in the person of the hero Fionn mac Cumhail, who acquired a magical thumb that, when sucked, would grant him knowledge. Two separate traditions tell us how he came by it, one of which is that his thumb was caught in the door of a faery mound. He had only to chew upon it, to know what he needed. Fionn uniquely combines the skills of a war-leader with the divinatory role of the poet; his gnawing upon the Thumb of Knowledge is a clear demonstration of the term *Teinm Laegda*. The following story, reveals how he used this skill:

> The fool of Fionn, grandson of Baiscni, was called Lomna the Lousy. One day Fionn went out hunting and Lomna stayed at home. There was a woman of the Luigne who slept with Fionn: in nearly every mountain and forest where Fionn and men roamed there was a woman in every region who was available to him. These were female innkeepers, ready to support the Fianna; for wherever they roamed, no-one would harm them. Fionn came into Tethba with his Fianna

and Lomna stayed behind. Lomna went walking and saw Cairpre, one of the Fianna, sleeping with Fionn's woman. Then the woman begged Lomna to say nothing. It felt dreadful to him to betray his master, so, when Fionn returned, Lomna cut an *ogham* inscription upon a four-sided stick, saying,

> 'A pole of wood within the
> champion's silver helmet.
> The husband of an adulterous whore is
> made fool of within the Fianna.
> There's some heather upon naked
> Ualann of the Luigne.'

And Fionn immediately understood this story and grew disgusted with the woman. But the woman knew that it was Lomna who had told him and she sent a messenger to Cairpre to come and kill the fool.

So Cairpre came and cut off Lomna's head and carried it off with him. Fionn returned to camp that evening and saw a body without a head. 'A body without a head,' said Fionn, 'let us discover whose it is.' And he put his thumb into his mouth and spoke through *teinm laegda*,

> 'It wasn't done by our folk,
> Nor by the Leinstermen,

No modesty has caused this,

No red dog has ravaged him,

No boar has torn him, nor eaten
   him, nor hidden him,

No secret what has befallen Lomna.'

'This is the body of Lomna,' said Fionn, 'and enemies have carried off his head.'

Then they unleashed the hounds and let them follow the scent. Fionn followed the track of the warriors and came upon Cairpre in an abandoned house, cooking fish upon a stone, and Lomna's head nearby the fire on a pole. The first serving that he cooked on the stone, Cairpre divided into twenty-seven portions, but he did not put a piece into the mouth of the head. Now this [lack of hospitality] was *geis* to the Fianna, and Lomna's head spoke, saying, 'A speckled, whitebellied salmon that has swum with lesser fish under the sea. I will not speak. I am no country pig who indiscriminately shits oak-mast everywhere. But I say that Cairpre has made a division that is unjust.' Which was the origin of this saying.

With the second serving, Cairpre divided the fish into another twenty-seven portions and the head said, 'You share an unjust portion at the second serving. A just judge would divide it differently, even though

I have no belly to digest it. The hatred of the Fianna will be upon Luigne.'

'Oh, throw out that head!' exclaimed Cairpre, 'since it heaps such abuse upon us.'

Then the head spoke again, 'At the first assault, the chieftain runs with his spear. You, yourself, will be jointed and divided and cut into collops. Fionn will bring fire and sword upon the Luigne now.'

And after that remark, Fionn came into that place and killed them.[5]

By chewing over the lay, Fionn discovers the dead man's name as it comes spontaneously springing to his lips. The obscurity of the *ogham* inscription is no trouble to Fionn, who successfully determines, by means of *phrase ogham* (*see* Glossary) that the alder stake in a palisade of silver denotes his own wife in her court; a sprig of hellebore in a bunch of cress means that her intentions are unwholesome; that the woman is his own wife and the place of her lover's assignation are conveyed by Lomna's message. Fionn then killed Cairpre and revenged himself upon the people of Luighne in Connacht, just as Lomna prophesied. Lomna's laconic post-mortem speech seems to employ a kind of *Teinm Laegda* of his own, as his oracular head backchats with his murderers, with typical Celtic black humour.

Here is another instance of the method from *Cormac's Glossary*, where the poet Maen deduces information about some bones in a short quatrain and, by so doing, the identity of the hound, whose name means 'Speed's Servant', leaps to his lips.

This was the time when Ailill Flann was King of Munster and Cormac mac Conn was King of Tara. They and Cairpre began to argue over the possession of the lapdog. And this is the way that the dispute was settled: the dog was to stay with each of them for a period of time. After this decision, the bitch gave birth to three puppies and they each had one: from this litter descend all the lapdogs of Ireland. And long after the original dog had died, it was Connla, son of Tadhg, son of Cian, son of Oilill Olum who found the lapdog's bare skull and took it as riddle to a poet, who had come with his composition to his father's house. The poet was Maen mac Edaine and Maen solved the riddle through *teinm laegda*, saying,

'Your pelt was smooth in Eogain's house,
In Conn's house there was food enough,
Your fair shape so admired
Before your beauty died in Cairpre's dwelling.
Mug-éime! This head is that of Mug-éime,
the very first lapdog ever brought to Ireland.'[6]

Fionn mac Cumhail is even said to have had foreknowledge of the coming of Christianity by means of *teinm laegda*, for he sat upon the Stone of the Hundreds in Munster and put his thumb between his teeth, and heaven and earth were revealed to him, although with knowledge of God and of the coming of Adze-Head (Patrick).[7] *Teinm Laegda* spirals into the unknown by means of the Inward Vision (p.34), until spontaneous verse discovers its source.

Dichetul Do Chennaib

Dichetul do Chennaib literally means 'Invocation or Spell on the Finger's Ends', a kind of spontaneous knowing that arrives when the sensitive touch-points of the *suile méare*, 'the eyes of the fingers', the whorls on the fingertips, touch something. Cormac says that 'the revelation comes directly from the tips of the poet's fingers'. Instantaneous knowledge flows into 'the pulse of poetry', which beats in a vein at the back of the brain, and out comes the information in poetic form. We have some good instances of this method, also from *Cormac's Glossary:*

> Coire Breccain [Corryvrekin], the great whirlpool that whirls between Ireland and Alba [Scotland], where many seas meet – the sea around Ireland at the north-west, the sea surrounding Alba at the

north-east, and the Irish sea between Ireland and Alba from the south. Like a pair of compasses, they whirl about, changing the waters between them turn and turn about like a millwheel until they are sucked down into the depths, leaving the opening like a cauldron with its gaping mouth. It could suck the whole of Ireland into its gaping maw. It vomits out great water spouts with thunderous belches as high as the clouds, just like the boiling of a cauldron over the fire.

Breccán, son of Main, son of Niall of the Nine Hostages, had fifty curraghs trading between Ireland and Alba, but one of them was drawn into the cauldron and none of the crew survived, so no news was ever heard about its sinking. No-one knew what had become of them until the blind poet, Lugaid, arrived at Bangor and his people walked along the beach of Inver Béce and found the clean skull of a dog and brought it to Lugaid. They asked him whose it was and he told them to lay it down so that he could touch it with the end of his poet's staff and made a *Dichetul do Chennaib* upon it, saying, 'This is the skull of Breccán's dog. It is the merest remnant of someone much greater for Breccán himself drowned among his people in this whirlpool.'[8]

Blind Lugaid doesn't even have to touch the skull with his fingers, only with the end of his staff to make his findings. *Dichetul do Chennaib* seems to have a strong element of psychometry, whereby the history of an object can be discovered by merely touching it. Some texts speak of a poet's ability to touch someone with his staff or to pick up an object and, by means of ritual invocation, to discover the history of that person or object, as in *The Exile of the Sons of Uisnech* where the host of Ulster is being served with food by the wife of Fedlimid. She is pregnant, and as she passes through the hall, the child cries out in her womb. At this shriek the company arose in terror, but the woman asks the druid, Cathbad, to give her an augury about this cry. Laying a hand on her belly, Cathbad pronounces:

> It is a woman who hath given that shriek,
> Golden haired, with long tresses, and tall,
> For whose love chieftains shall strive …
> O Deirdruí! thou are great cause of ruin;
> Though famous, and fair and pale:
> Before Fedlimid's daughter shall part from life,
> All Ulster shall wail her deeds.[9]

The meeting of two poets sometimes resulted in a quick exchange of *Dichetul do Chennaib*, as each strove to divine the antecedents of the other by holding onto the other's staff, in a poetic cross-divination. Bradford Keeney who has worked among the San

Bushman of the Kalahari writes of such meetings, which may help illuminate what is happening:

> When a Kalahari shaman meets another shaman, the arrows [of energy] flow from heart to heart. They make an instant connection that validates who they are. This moment of connection feels like tingling electricity and often results in a shout being released. The same thing happens when two people seasoned in the spirit meet. Their hearts send out vibrations that penetrate the spiritual veil.[10]

It is the very piercing of this veil that the *filidh* were about when they used the Three Illuminations. But did they learn this skill from an earlier, ancestral tradition?

Ancestral Oracles and the Venerated Head

From this brief encounter with the Three Illuminations, it is evident that many of the examples of *Dichetul do Chennaib* given by Cormac concern the finding of information from the bones of the dead and the revelation of their long-forgotten stories.

There is a long tradition of ancestral veneration among the islands of Britain and Ireland. In prehistoric times, bodies of the dead often received two kinds of rites: first, the defleshing of their bones, and secondly, their removal to a place of veneration.

Megalithic and earlier traditions of curating ancestral bones or remains by organizing them in chambered tombs, show that excarnated bodies were arranged in their different bone groups – leg and arm bones, skulls etc. The excavations of Cladh Hallan, on South Uist in the Western Isles of Scotland, revealed a tradition of venerating special ancestors by mummifying them first, either in peat or by wind drying. Some bodies revealed a time lapse of 600 years between death and eventual burial, suggesting that the mummies had been ceremonially displayed.[11] With named and known individuals, their funeral rites no doubt involved the telling of a person's deeds in the form of a paean, with keening and funeral games.

The theologian Tertullian, in his *A Treatise On the Soul* 57, relates: 'The Celts also … spend the night near the tombs of their famous men,' to receive oracles and visions.[12] This tradition was clearly still operative among the Gauls' cousins across the sea, and continued around the northwest coasts of Europe as an accepted means of gaining ancestral wisdom, especially in the Norse version of *útiseta* or 'outsitting'.

The *Book of Lecan* tells us about Irish burial customs:

> A *fert* [a mound made of stones] of
>   one door for a man of science,
>
> A *fert* of two doors upon a woman.
>
> A *fert* with doors also for boys
>   and maidens,

> *Cnocs* [hill-mounds] on
>> distinguished foreigners
>
> *Murs* upon those dying of plague.[13]

A *fert* is understood to have been a vaulted grave-mound of stones over which earth was laid. But why a mound with doors? Could these be in order to allow egress or access? A *mur* was an enclosed bank, since it was important to ensure that no-one accidentally opened a plague pit and became infected.

The interment of the first body into the ground of a newly settled place was considered to be a solemn, foundation burial, which made the deceased into a 'way-shower' ancestor, who could speak from the ancestral realms to the community by way of oracle. The story is told of the first settlement of Iona where St Columcille said to his brothers:

> 'It would be well for us that our roots should pass into the earth here. It is permitted to you that some one of you go under the earth of this island to consecrate it.' Odhran arose quickly and thus spake: 'If you accept me,' said he, 'I am ready for that.' 'O Odhran,' said Columcille, 'you shall receive the reward of this; no request shall be granted to any one at my tomb unless he first ask of thee.' Odhran then went to heaven.[14]

Odhran, upon rising from the grave, utters: 'Hell is not as bad as it's reported.' To which Columcille rejoins: 'Clay, clay upon Odhran', in case he should say too much! Columcille's purpose is evidently to deny Odhran the liberty of becoming an ancestral oracle!

Odhran's interment sanctifies the ground for human occupation, but his sacrifice is primarily to create an 'ancestral hot-line', which will be available to all who subsequently inhabit that site. Odhran's body consecrates the soil of Iona, while his soul remains watchful and able to grant petitions – a primacy which is not accorded to St Columcille. Odhran remains watchful down the centuries, gathering to himself a company of the most renowned Scottish kings and nobles, as well as the holy monks of the Iona foundation. His story gives us insight into the process of ancestral inauguration.

There are innumerable accounts in which stories are retrieved by persons who visit tombs and listen to the ancestors who arise from them. The most famous is the rediscovery of the *Táin Bó Cúailgne*, the Cattle Raid of Cooley, told in a story from the Book of Leinster. It relates how none of the poets of Ireland in the time of Senchán Torpeist (d. AD 647) remember more than a few fragments of the Raid, and so Emine and Murgen mac Senchán go to sit at the memorial stone in Connacht of Fergus mac Róice, one of the great Ulster heroes, and sing to his spirit. Fergus's spirit arises and relates the whole of the Raid from end to end, so that the story returns to living memory once again.[15]

In the 12th-century Irish *Accalam na Senórach*, or *The Colloquy of the Ancients*, a similar account is given to

St Patrick, who goes about Ireland with two ancient heroes of the Fianna – Oisín mac Fionn mac Cumhail and Caílte mac Crondchú. They delve into the ancestral memory of Ireland by visiting different places in the land, speaking to the faeryfolk of the *sí*, relating stories about past deeds of heroes and excavating long-lost treasures in a wild kind of ancestral road movie. When the Fenian heroes have fulfilled their mission and the poets of Ireland have preserved all their sayings, the men of Ireland assemble to learn them also.[16] St Patrick asks the heroes what has kept them alive for so long and they respond: 'The truth of our hearts, the strength of our arms and the constancy of our tongues.'[17]

This form of ancestral retrieval offered a continuous vision of wisdom, a kind of ancestral oracle. Unlike the present generation, which sees the ancestors as 'dead and gone', the Celts understood their ancestors to be perpetual sources of wisdom. They were the voice of the tribe, speaking with collective authority, beyond that of the living. This understanding originates in the druidic belief in metempsychosis, whereby living beings passed into the forms of other beings. Both Fintan mac Bochra and Tuan Mac Carill are the source of all Irish history, having lived through the ages in the forms of different animals, but maintaining a constant, living memory in each successive form until they are both reborn as men.[18] The title for this round of lives was called the *tuirgin*, which *Cormac's Glossary* defines as:

A birth that passes from every nature into another, i.e. a birth of the true nature … As Fachtna son of Senchaid says: 'he gives a transitory birth which has traversed all nature from Adam and goes through every wonderful time down to the world's doom. He gives the nature of one life … to the last person who shall be on the verge of judgement.'[19]

We've seen how bones can speak with the voice of the ancients, but why did the Celtic peoples hold the human head in such veneration? The 3rd-century AD Gaulish temple of Roquepertuse, north of Marseilles, has a portico with niches, in which human heads taken in battle were placed, bespeaking horrific blood-thirstiness. There are many historical and literary accounts in British and Irish lore, of warriors taking the heads of their enemies and preserving them. For the Celts, the head was the seat of wisdom and of the soul. To venerate the heads of one's forebears was only a form of proper ancestral respect. To take the heads of one's enemies was to appropriate their cunning and wisdom for the use of one's own tribe, and to deny that wisdom to the enemy. As we've seen from the example of Lomna, whose head speaks after death, the oracular head is a source of wisdom.

The seeming obsession with ancestral remains may be illuminated by a 15th-century Irish text that reveals one of the ancient doctrines concerning the soul. Three cauldrons or subtle vessels are believed to be the receptacles of the soul: they are located in the belly, the breast and the head. The cauldron of the belly is called *Coire Goriath* 'the cauldron of warming', which maintains the life of the body; the cauldron of the chest is called *Coire Ernmae* or 'the cauldron of (vocational) gifts'; while the cauldron of the head is called *Coire Sois* (a contraction of *So-Fhios* or 'Very Wise'), which is 'the cauldron of wisdom'.[20] The wisdom that resides in the skull is the supreme wisdom, the kind of knowledge that poets were seeking through the Three Illuminations.

The whole body was regarded as a microcosm of the greater wisdom that shone in the darkness; by the light of the soul, all that was unknown might be known, through the ancestral oracle and through the Three Illuminations that spoke the language of the *gléfiosa*.

Shining Light upon the Unknown

Whatever is mysterious to you is capable of illumination, if you take it with you into the darkness of the 'vein of poetry'. Sit still somewhere in solitude, such as on a beach or on a moor or a hillside, then use your palms to cover your eyes.

Without exercising your rational function or trying to find a solution by ordinary means, take the matter into your soul and let it sit there. Make your own invocation, in your own words, for illumination and help to uncover what is needful to know. Speak or sing the words aloud and mean them, let them resonate, just as a stone drops into the pool and sends its ripples running.

In the half-dreaming of your stillness, many immediate thoughts or impressions will arise. If you are outside, the elements, the weather or animals may be part of your findings; do not exclude them as irrelevant. Be aware of the phosphenes that dance behind your eyes when you press your palms over them; their dancing is the pattern of the shapers, the spirits that attend this art. You may be caught up into that dance, or it may come inside you, deepening your understanding.

For your first trial, find a stone nearby and pick it up. Hold it in your hand and try *Dichetul do Chennaib* for yourself: what is the stone's story, what does it tell you? Tell it as a story. For your second trial, hold the stone and speak or sing aloud the stream of ideas arising from it, in verse form or chant: that is your *Teinm Laegda*. For your third trial, hold the stone and wrap yourself up in your coat or shawl and lie down – on your back or side. Be aware of the light that is within the stone becoming larger until it encompasses you. Listen, feel, taste the story that it tells you. This knowing is your *Imbas Forosna*.

Ensure that the subject of your seeking doesn't overlook someone else's business, or isn't knowledge that you can't live with: as is often said, those who look into matters that don't concern them, often find a distortion of themselves.

CHAPTER 6

Fate, Destiny and the Sovereignty of the Soul

I swear a destiny upon you that your side will
touch no wife until you obtain Olwen.

Culhwch ac Olwen

The *Tarbh Feis* and the *Geasa*

No area of seership and prophecy was more important for the peace of the land than a clear succession. If the rightful king was not identified and inaugurated speedily, many claimants might disrupt the peace by internecine conflict. Celtic rulers did not succeed by primogeniture but by tribal election of the most suitable candidate, drawn from the royal blood lineage; in this way, a child or young man would not receive the responsibility, but rather a mature man from the tribal kinship group. The nature of a king determined the kind of reign that he would have, for his character could influence the bounty of the harvest, the fertility of the soil and sea, and whether the land would be peaceful or at war. For the same reason, a maimed king was instantly disqualified from rule, as happened when Nuadu lost his hand in battle and was replaced by Lugh Lamhfada.

The selection and election of sovereigns was an onerous duty, which devolved to druids and vision-poets, since only the seer might discover the candidate's mystical suitability. The ancient way of establishing kingship in an uncertain succession, was by the use of the *tarbh-feis* or 'bull-ceremony'. The *tarbh-feis* was a form of sacrifice and incubation ceremony, very like the performance of *Imbas Forosna* (*see* p.94). A bull was killed, and its flesh was boiled up in a cauldron. The druid who was to perform the incubation 'ate his fill of the bull's meat and drank of its broth,' and was wrapped in the bull's flayed hide, bloody side nearest the skin, 'and a spell of truth was chanted over him in his bed. Whoever he saw in his sleep would be king and the dreamer would be killed if he uttered a lie.'[1] The *tarbh feis* was still being enacted in the Western Isles of Scotland in the 17th century, according to Martin Martin:

> The second way of consulting the oracle was by a party of men who first retired to solitary places, remote from any house, and there they singled out one of their number, and wrapt him in a big cow's hide, which they folded about him; his whole body was covered with it except his head, and so left in this posture all night until his invisible friends relieved him by giving a proper answer to the question in hand, which he received, as he fancied, from several persons that he found about him all that time. His consorts returned to him at break of day, and then he communicated his news to them, which often proved fatal to those concerned in such unwarrantable enquiries. … Mr. Alexander Cooper, present minister of North Uist, told me that one John Erach, in the isle of Lewis assured him it was his fate to have been led by his curiosity with some who consulted this oracle, and that he was to spend a night within the hide, as above mentioned; during which time he felt and heard such terrible

things that he could not express them: the impression
it made on him was such as could never go off, and he
said that for a thousand worlds he would never again
be concerned in the like performance, for this had
disordered him to a high degree.[2]

The *tarbh-feis* is described in the Irish story of Conaire, from the
Destruction of Da Derga's Hostel – a cautionary story for kings –
relating how important it is for rulers to keep their contractual
promises and obligations. It also demonstrates the nature of the
geis or *geasa* (pl).

Conaire's mother, Mess Buachalla, 'the cowherd's fosterchild',
was the daughter of Cormac of Ulster and Etain. Cormac desired
that this baby should be abandoned by being left in a pit, but
compassionate cowherds took her away into the land of Eterscel
of Tara, and secretly fostered her themselves. Hidden away in her
secret hut, she grew in beauty. But King Eterscel's spies looked
in upon her and reported back to him. Eterscel was childless. It
had been prophesied that a woman of unknown race would bear
him a son and he determined to marry her. But before she could
be brought to him, she was visited by an otherworldly being.
Through the skylight of her room, a bird flew in, dropped his
bird-skin on the floor and slept with her. He told her afterwards
that the king was coming to wreck her house and carry her away,
but that she would bear a son by her bird-man, a boy who must
never kill birds and that he was to be named Conaire. Eterscel

took Mess Buachalla as his wife and, believing Conaire to be his natural son, sent him to be fostered by a great champion.

At Eterscel's death, a *tarbh-feis* was instituted to discern the true kingly successor. At the same time that the bull-feaster was in his incubation, Conaire was visited by one of his otherworldly father's bird-people, Nemhglan ('the Clear Heavens'), who told him to go straight away, stark-naked to Tara with only a stone and sling in his hand. All the way along the road, he was led by birds, which he attempted to kill with his sling, until the birds left off their shape and became faery men who tried to kill him. Nemhglan shielded Conaire, reminding him again that he was not to kill or molest birds, because they were his relations.

Ahead of Conaire, upon the Tara road, three kings waited holding clothes and ready to greet him, because the druid bull-feaster's vision foretold a stark-naked man on the Tara road was the true king. The people of Tara were aghast at the sight, saying, 'Surely our bull feast and the spell of truth have failed, for it is only a young, beardless lad that we have envisioned!' But Conaire responds, 'It is no disgrace for a young, generous king like me to take the kingship, since the guarantee of Tara is mine by right, through my father and grandfather.'[3]

The *geis* can best be described as the contract with one's destiny and gifts, requiring that one keep faith with or refrain from committing the actions outlined in its clauses. These might include positive injunctions or negative prohibitions binding upon an individual. *Geasa* go with the territory or the job description, sometimes given at birth or upon accession, as things that must be done or not done; unbreakable rules that support or destroy personal or territorial honour if not maintained. Heroes, like the Irish Cú Chulainn, have their special *geasa*, but kings come with more *geasa* than any other people because more is required from those to whom more is given. The hero, Fionn mac Cumhaill's *geasa* meant that he should not go across the Moor of Brega in the morning, nor might he avoid the company of poets; he was not to sleep with his wife Sadb on midsummer night, nor to travel to Slievenamon at Beltane; he could not look upon a dead man not killed by weapons.[4]

Geasa are also placed upon an individual as he assumes responsibility, like the long list of kingly obligations that Conaire assumes on his inauguration; but some are also born with a person, as we see from Conaire's *geis* to not kill birds because his father's kindred take this form. Another way of understanding *geasa* is as the contract of the individual soul with life: they maintain the basis for balanced behaviour, they uphold the gifts and skills of an individual and they ensure that it is kept safe. The breaking of a *geis* is an immediate endangering of the soul, a violation of one's nature.

At Conaire's inauguration, Nemhglan returns to utter a series of onerous *geasa,* which restrict the king's freedom and which form part of his contract of kingship between the land and the otherworld.

Your reign will be subject to a restriction, but your bird-reign will be noble, for these are your *geasa*: You shall not go *deasil* [sunwise] around Tara not *tuathal* [widdershins] around Mag Breg. You must not hunt the beasts of Cerna. You shall not go out every ninth night beyond Tara. You shall not sleep in a house from which firelight or light can be seen from outside after sunset. Three Reds shall not precede you into Red's house. No rapine is allowed during your reign. After sunset, a company of one woman or one man shall enter the house where you lodge. You shall not settle the dispute between two of your slaves.[5]

The nine *geasa* of Conaire are, needless to say, broken in every point, one by one, until he stubbornly decides to go into the hostel of Da Derga (Two Reds) of Leinster. As he is about to enter, three red-clad horsemen precede him into the hostel. But worse is to follow once they are inside, as the *geasa* tumble:

They saw a lone woman coming to the door of the Hostel, after sunset, asking to be let in. As long as a weaver's beam was each of her two shins, and they were dark as the back of a stag-beetle. A greyish, woolly mantle she wore. Her pubic hair hung down to her knee. Her lips were on one side of her head. She came and put one of her shoulders against the door-post of the house, casting the evil eye on the king and the youths who surrounded him in the Hostel. He himself spoke to her from within.

'Well, O woman,' says Conaire, 'if you're a seer, what do you see for us?'

'Truly I see for you,' she said, 'that neither hide nor hair of you shall escape from the place into which you've come, except what the birds will bear away in their claws.'

'It was not an evil omen we asked, woman,' he said: 'you are not our customary augurer. What is your name, woman?'

'Cailb,' she answers.

'That is not much of a name,' says Conaire.

'I have many more names besides.'

'What are they?' asks Conaire.

'Easy to say,' said she. 'Samon, Sinand, Seisclend, Sodb, Caill, Coll, Díchóem, Dichiúil, Díthím, Díchuimne, Dichruidne, Dairne, Dáríne, Déruaine, Egem, Agam, Ethamne, Gním, Cluiche, Cethardam, Níth, Némain, Nóennen, Badb, Blosc, B[l]oár, Huae, óe Aife la Sruth, Mache, Médé, Mod.'

On one foot, and holding up one hand, and breathing one breath she sang all those names to them from the door of the house.

'I swear by the gods of my tribe,' says Conaire, 'that I will call you by none of these names whether I lodge here a long or a short time.'

'What's your desire?' says Conaire.

'That which you also desire,' she answered.

'It's a *geis* of mine,' says Conaire, 'to receive the company of one woman after sunset.'

'Though it be your *geis*,' she replied, 'I will not go until I'm invited in at once this very night.'

'Tell her,' says Conaire, 'that an ox and a bacon-pig shall be taken out to her, and my leavings: provided that she stays tonight in some other place.'

'If it's true that such a thing has befallen, that the king has no room in his house to give a lone woman a meal and bed, they will be received by someone with generosity – for the hospitality of the Prince in the Hostel has departed.'[6]

Conaire is shamed into admitting Cailb or 'Spear', the woman whose many names are a roll call of land features and faery beings, signalling that she is the announcer of extraordinary deeds. She stands cursing him in the attitude of *corrguinacht*, the crane's posture, cancelling one hand, one foot and one eye. (By putting away one half of the body, one is cancelling or hiding it from ordinary reality, so that it appears in the otherworld to give strength to the curse.) Around the hostel are gathering a number of Conaire's enemies and rebels who conspire to bring about the king's death, including a one-eyed British pirate loyal to Conaire's grandfather. The hostel is attacked and Conaire dies in the conflict, foresworn of every *geasa* he once promised to keep.

Interestingly, Irish lore associated the *tarbh feis* with the imposition of *geasa* upon spirits in order to obtain information. In this account by Geoffrey Keating in his 17th-century *History of Ireland*, we learn that the act of divining has itself become synonymous with great effort:

> Many are the ways in which [the druids] laid *geasa* upon [demons]: such as to keep looking at their own images in water, or gazing on the clouds of heaven, or keep listening to the noise of the wind or the chattering of birds. But when all these expedients failed them, and they were obliged to do their utmost, what they did was, to make round wattles of the quicken [rowan] tree, and to spread thereon the hides of the bulls offered in sacrifice, putting the side which had been next the flesh uppermost, and thus relying on their *geasa* to summon the demons to get information from them, as the conjurer does nowadays in the circus; whence the old saw has since been current which says that one has *gone on his wattles of knowledge* [*cliabtaich fis*] when he has done his utmost to obtain information.[7]

The rowan tree was one of the paramount trees of the druids, still retaining its magical lore in Celtic countries to this day, as a wood that either protects against sorcery or one which enchanters use in their rites.

Contracts of the Soul

As we have seen, rulers do not govern solely by virtue of their power, army or kindred. There are unseen contract-holders whose authority outranks any king: these are the divinities and spirits of the land, who may appear as mighty beings like Flaitheas, the goddess of sovereignty; or who patrol the land as one of the *si*, the faery folk. These beings are the ones that determine who will rule and how it is done. Each locality has its own tutelary spirits, which make different demands upon those rulers whom they endorse. The contractual small-print of every king is specific and local to the region governed, and is laid down in order to respect boundaries and avoid giving offence to those who have allowed them to rule.

Flaitheas, the goddess of sovereignty, appears in many Celtic stories from Niall of the Nine Hostages through to the medieval stories of 'The Wedding of Sir Gawain and Dame Ragnell' and Chaucer's 'The Wife of Bath's Tale'. Her initial appearance is generally as an ugly hag; only those who truly honour her will perceive her true likeness, just as only a courageous and responsible candidate will volunteer to rule a country well, despite its problems. A story from the Middle Irish *Coir Anmann* or *Fitness of Names* tell how Lughaidh Laidhe Maicniadh and his brothers encounter her:

> Why were the five sons of Daire Domthigh all called Lughaidh? Not hard to say why. It had been

prophesied that one of his sons would take the sovereignty of Eire, and that Lughaidh would be his name, and so each son was named Lughaidh. At the celebration of Tailltin Fair, Daire's five sons competed in horsemanship; and the Druid said, 'What good are your sons, since only one of them shall assume the monarchy of Eire.'

Daire asked him: 'What son shall take the sovereignty after me?'

'A golden fawn shall arrive at the fair,' said the Druid, 'and the son who shall overtake it is the one who shall succeed you.'

As soon as the golden fawn arrived at the fair, the men of Eire pursued it and the sons of Daire followed it to Beann Eadair where a magical mist rose between them and the men of Eire. The sons of Daire pursued it onward to Dal-Meascorb in Leinster, and the first Lughaidh overtook the fawn, while his brother Lughaidh flayed its skin and became called Lughaidh Cosc [Slaughterer]. Afterwards a great snow fell, so that it was hard work for them to carry or hold their arms. One Lugaidh went in search of shelter, and found a large house with a great fire burning, with abundant food and drink, dishes of silver and beds of *findruine* [white silver]. And in the middle of the house stood a large hideous hag.

'Young man, what do you seek?' she asked. 'Only a bed till morning,' he replied. The hag said, 'Well, if you will come into my bed tonight, you shall have one.' And the youth said that he would rather not, and he returned to his brothers. 'You have refused the sovereignty and monarchy,' she said after him.

The other brothers went in after him in turn. She asked them each why he had come, and the first said he'd come for a wild hog, and that he could eat it all by himself. 'Lughaidh Orca [Pig] shall be your name among your tribe,' said she.

She asked the same of the next and he said, 'Nothing. I was chosen, but I fell asleep.'

'That was sleepy. So Lughaidh Cal [Sleepy] shall be your name among the tribe,' said she.

She asked the next. 'A wild fawn showed itself to me,' said he. 'Lughaidh Laidhe [the Strong] shall be your name among your tribe.'

Another brother came to her and she asked him. 'I have eaten what they've left,' said he. 'Lughaidh Corb [Corpse] shall be your name,' said she, 'for corrupt is the thing you have taken.'

The last Lugaidh was asked the same question. 'I met an ox and devoured it alone,' he said. 'Lughaidh Laidhe Maicniadh [Strong Progeny] shall be your name among your tribe.'

This is how they got their names. At length Lughaidh Laidhe Maicniadh went with her into the house for food and drink. After this the hag lay down in the bed of *findruine*, and Maicniadh lay down after her in the bed, and it seemed to him that the light of her face was as the sun rising in the month of May, and the fragrance of her was as the smell of a flower garden.

After this he made love to her, and she said, 'Good is your journey, for I am Sovereignty, and you shall obtain Eire or one descended from you shall.' They afterwards took new meats and old drinks, and cups were distributed to them alone, and he lived with the Sovereignty. On waking in the morning, they found themselves without house or fire except the bare mountainside, and their hounds were tied to their lances. They returned to Tailltin Fair, and told the story of their adventures.[8]

In the last passage, the distribution of cups has a significance that might be overlooked, did we not know from stories like the *Baile in Scail* or 'the Phantom's Prophecy' that it is Flaitheas who pours out drink to the acclaimed king. Lugaidh Laidhe Maicniadh alone is prepared to sleep with the hag and so he enters into a contract with Sovereignty, and experiences her transformation into her lovely form.

Flaitheas' act of naming each of the Lugaidh brothers from

the nature of his deeds derives from the Irish custom of giving a child a childhood name. The adult name would be revealed when subsequent deeds manifested the innate individuality. Thus, in the Ulster Cycle, the young boy Setanta, with all his venturesome and prodigious deeds, decides to join the company of the King of Ulster. When he and all his men are already feasting in the hall of Culainn, and the dogs have been turned loose to guard the fort, Setanta, nothing daunted, wrestles with the biggest hound until he overcomes it. The men of Ulster emerge to see what is happening and Culainn complains about the loss of his hound. Cathbad the druid announces that Setanta must make good the loss by becoming Culainn's guard-dog himself, and that he must now be called Cú Chulainn or 'the Hound of Culainn'. This name is prophetically recapitulated when, after the Ulstermen have been smitten by the *noinend*, a curse set by the dying Macha upon nine generations of Ulster that they become as weak as a woman in childbed at their time of greatest need, Cú Chulainn stands in the pass as the sole combatant to defend the borders of Ulster.[9]

Similarly, when Rhiannon's long-lost son, stolen from her side as a baby, returns as a small boy, in *Pwyll, Prince of Dyfed,* she exclaims 'At last my trouble is over', and a nearby elder proclaims that the boy be called Pryderi or 'Anxiety'. When she protests against this name, the elder reminds her it is only fitting that the boy be named from his mother's first relieved utterance.[10] It is a name that Pryderi amply fulfils in his later youth, as he first becomes stuck in the otherworld and then is duped by Gwydion ap Don into giving up the pigs that were the token of his family's contract with Pen Annwyfn, the Lord of the Underworld.

There is a clear link between names and their owner's contract with life. We can see this if we look at the Irish word for 'soul' (*anam*), and the Irish word for 'name' (*ainm*) that has the same pronunciation. Our name and our soul are closely bound together. Within each of us lie the seeds of our potential and destiny. Our fate is a different matter, since we are the physical result of our parent's union, and we inherit our frame and certain tribal tendencies from our ancestors. This is expressed in *The Three Cauldrons*, a 15th-century Irish tract about the contracts between the poet and his poetry, but which tells us more about the contracts of the soul:

> Question: is the source of poetic art in a person's body or soul? Some say the soul, since the body is one with it. Others say the body, since it stems from a fitting source, from father and grandfather, but it is truer to say that the source of poetic art is in each person's body, though in every second person it is absent.[11]

It goes on to describe three cauldrons that reside in the body and which constitute the vessels of the soul. The lower cauldron, *Coire Goiriath* or 'Cauldron of Warming' maintains the health of the body and remains upright until we are dead. This lower one is the container of our fate – something that none of us can seriously change or alter, for we cannot change where we were born, or to whom, or alter our physical appearance and dispositions. The middle cauldron, *Coire Ernmae* or 'Cauldron of Vocation' whose meaning includes 'a course of action, an apprenticeship or a vocational tendency', is connected to the way we use and develop our personal gifts. The top cauldron *Coire Sois* (p.111) or 'the Cauldron of Knowledge', is connected to the spiritual inspiration whose influences develop our potential. The top two cauldrons can move and, in people whose gifts are undeveloped or who suffer emotional turmoil, they can turn over so that those individuals remain fixated on merely everyday affairs, or else enter a depressive phase where no inspiration can move them. Whoever doesn't interact with their destiny is doomed to live according to their fate alone, unless they choose to engage with it.

These three cauldrons are clearly connected strongly to our soul's contract with life, and with the manner in which some people seem tuned into seership and vision, while others are disinterested, repelled or even frightened by the prospect of perceiving more than everyday reality. As we have seen (p.111) the upper cauldron is associated with the head, while the middle one resides in the upper torso and the lower one in the lower torso. When all cauldrons are upright, there is a clear alignment of the powers of our fate and destiny with the inspirational otherworldly powers who mentor us in a way that nourishes our lives beyond the merely normal.

While seers can sometimes perceive a person's fate and sometimes also the seeds of their destiny, traditionally the bestowal of personal gifts and talents belongs to the spirits who oversee each soul. In pan-Celtic lore, these beings are the *Garmengabiae*, or the Gifting Mothers, we know them better today as the faery godmothers. The *Garmengabiae* are related to the early Irish goddess Carman, whose name is taken from *garman* or 'a weaver's beam'.[12] They are the Celtic equivalent of the Greek *Moirae* or the Fates, who spin the thread, weave the fabric and cut it from the loom of life. Many Romano-Celtic statutes of the Gifting Mothers are found across Europe; they are most often shown as three goddesses of similar age or as a maiden, mother and grandmother; some sit with fruits and bread in their lap, while others hold babies, cornu-copias and abundance. The British faeries are significantly entitled *Bendith y Mamau* or The Mothers' Blessing; they are frequently accompanied by three small, hooded men who are known as the *Genii Cucullati* or Hooded Spirits, who often carry eggs.

The Gifting Mothers are shared by both Celtic and Rhineland peoples.

Saxo Germanicus tells a story about the Danish king, Fridleif, who took his three-year-old son, Olaf, into the house of the gods to pray to 'three maidens sitting on three seats'. The first two granted him the gifts of charm and generosity, but the third said that he would nonetheless be niggardly in his giving.[13] Fridleif's temple visit tells us that the Gifting Mothers, or their priestesses who speak oracularly on their behalf, bestow gifts or single out and bless innate qualities that his young son possesses.

When taken together, the Gifting Mothers and the Hooded Spirits who wait upon them, are deeply involved with the creation of life and the awakening of individual gifts. The Mothers bestow gifts upon each soul – just as at Sleeping Beauty's birth, in the folk story – while the Hooded Ones in their phallic hooded cloaks are involved with the transmission of life.

Throughout the Celtic world, we come across accounts of the Nine Sisters, who are a widespread variation on the Gifting Mothers; just as the classical triplicity of the Fates also surfaces as a ninefold gathering of the Muses. The 1st-century Roman geographer, Pomponius Mela, wrote about a Gaulish sisterhood in his *De Situ Orbis III,* 6,48:

> The island of Sein, near the Ossimiens, is known because of the oracle of a Gaulish God; the priestesses of that divinity are nine in number; the Gauls call them *Senes* [the Old Ones]; they believe that, animated by a particular spirit, they can by their spells create storms in the air and on the sea, take the appearance of any sort of animal, cure the most serious illnesses, know and foretell the future, but only to those seamen who go over the ocean to see them.[14]

When the Dark Age Arthur makes his perilous descent to Annwfyn, the British underworld, in the 9th-century poem *Preiddeu Annwfyn*, he goes in search of a cauldron 'ridged with enamel, rimmed with pearl', as his chief poet, Taliesin tells us:

> My original song stems from the cauldron,
>
> By the breath of nine maidens was it kindled.
>
> The Chief of Annwfyn's cauldron,
>   what is its power?[15]

The warming breath of the Nine Sisters is what kindles the cauldron, just as their breath warms the lower cauldron that puts life into an individual, and overturns the middle cauldron so that it fills with the gifts bestowed when we were born. It also brings to the boil the upper cauldron so that the inspiration spills out into the whole world and shares its gifts. The Nine Sisters are the potent Celtic muses who mentor and encourage every living being, and who also receive us back when life is ending.

When the medieval King Arthur is mortally wounded, he is ferried to the Island of Avalon, to be healed by the goddess Morgen, and her eight sisters, as related by Geoffrey of Monmouth:

> ... nine sisters rule by a pleasing set of laws those who come to them from our country. She who is first of them is more skilled in the healing art, and excels her sisters in the beauty of her person. Morgen is her

name, and she has learned what useful properties all the herbs contain, so that she can cure sick bodies. She also knows an art by which to change her shape, and to cleave the air on new wings like Daedelus; when she wishes she is at Brest, Chartres or Pavia, and when she wills, she slips down from the air onto your shores. And men say that she has taught mathematics to her sisters, Moronoe, Mazoe, Gliten, Glitonea, Cliton, Tyronoe, Thitis, Thetis best known for her cither.[17]

This healer Morgen is a keeper of the arts and gifts, not yet reframed as the evil enchantress Morgan le Fay by medieval clerics. In Morgen and her sisters we can still see a likeness to the original ninefold.

The spirits who attend on kings and heroes, also attend upon us, to bring out the skills and qualities that are required for the maintenance and shaping of the world. The Gifting Mothers and the Nine Sisters keep their protégés on track by means of the *geasa* that are given or bestowed at birth, and throughout life, so that fate can rise up from its mundane condition, fuse marvellously with our destiny, making our whole life into:

> a noble brew in which is boiled the
> stock of each knowledge,
>
> (becoming) an enduring power whose
> protection never ebbs …

Good is the confluence of power:
  it builds up strength.

It is greater than any domain, it is
  better than any inheritance.

It numbers us among the wise, and
  we depart from the ignorant.[17]

From within the cauldrons of the soul, the seer looks into the future to see the prophecies, omens and portents that are the signposts along the road ahead. What visions will we find?

Soul Shield Contracts

Each person has sovereignty over their soul, but do you know what are your soul's protective coverings, its *geasa*? With whatever gifts, talents and skills you have been endowed by the Nine Sisters or the Gifting Mothers, it is essential that you maintain your contract with them. Your *geasa* are the smallprint on that contract, ensuring the maintenance of your gifts and protecting you from dangers that might overwhelm you. All skills require practice as a minimum requirement, but what other things must you perform, or not engage in, to keep them alive? Our *geasa* are our soul-shields, not for sharing with others unless it is to keep us alive. Look closely at your position in life as an individual, a friend and family member, a citizen and inhabitant of your land, as a living soul. What duties are incumbent upon you? What promises, oaths and conditions maintain you in these positions? What must you keep inviolable? What maintains your skills and gifts, and enables the universe to be inspired? Some of these conditions may be laid upon you already, some you may have taken upon yourself; they may change as you take on, or leave off, certain roles in your community, but never doubt that these *geasa* are the keys to your honour. Burnish them as your armour, but never try to banish them as a curse, for they are what keep your life and soul together. They are the binding contract between you and your land, between you and your inspirers, between you and your very soul.

CHAPTER 7

The Prophetic Vision

The druids Lucru and Lucet Maol prophesied:

'Adzehead will come over wild seas,

his mantle hole-headed, his staff crook-headed,

his table in the back part of his house.

He chants impiety from the front of his house,

all of his household will answer "Amen, Amen".

Thesaurus Paleohibernicus

Druidic Prophecy

One of the most famous Irish prophecies concerning the coming of St Patrick, stems from the mouths of druids – or does it? Patrick's nickname among the Irish was Tálcend or 'Axe-head' due to his mitre, yet his chasuble and his bishop's crook, his altar and his prayers are all alluded to in this prophecy by druids who have not yet seen him. This is probably a prophecy after the event, put into the mouths of druids to help to support the inevitability of Christianization – a common theme in Irish lore.

Prophetic knowledge of the coming of Christ was even incorporated into the Ulster Cycle, whose action is cited to be contemporaneous with his crucifixion. We hear how Cét mac Mágach loosed a shot made of the petrified brains of Mesgegra, King of Leinster, which embedded itself in the head of King Conchobor of Ulster. For the next seven years, Conchobor lived a careful life, mindful of the advice of his druids that any undue excitement would kill him, until a certain day when:

> Conchobor was at a gathering the day that Christ was crucified, and the nobles of the men of Ireland were about him. When darkness came upon the sun, and the moon turned the colour of blood, Conchobor asked Cathbad what was wrong with the elements. 'Your foster-brother,' he said, 'the man who was born

on the same night as you, he is now undergoing martyrdom, and he has been put on the cross, and that is what that thing portends.' 'Well then,' said Conchobor, 'I will kill a thousand men to rescue Christ!' and he seized his two spears and shook them so violently that they broke in his hands. He drew his sword and attacked the woods around him until it was an empty plain, which is now Mag Lamraige in Fir Ros. 'If I could reach them, this is how I would avenge Christ on the Jews and those who have crucified him.' His fury caused Mesgegra's brain to burst out of his head, and his own brain with it, and he died.[1]

We have few authenticated druidic prophecies, but Flavius Vopiscus of Syracuse gives a roughly contemporaneous prophecy about Diocletian who, when he was but a common soldier, stayed at an inn in the Gaulish region of Tongri. His hostess was a druidess, and when it came time to pay the bill, he paid just the bare minimum, leaving no tip. On being challenged for his meaness, Diocletian replied that he would be more generous when he became emperor. The druidess replied, 'Do not laugh, Diocletian, for when you have slain the Boar, you will indeed be Emperor.' Diocletian must have often looked to see his fortune every time he hunted boar, but the prophecy only came about after he had killed the prefect Arrius, who was nicknamed 'the Boar'. Diocletian was emperor between AD 284 and 305.[2] For a Gaulish druidess to deliver this prophecy in a suspiciously late era, well after Gaul's Roman conquest, it is to be wondered again whether a certain amount of arcane 'set-dressing' has been employed to give authenticity to an imperial *fait accompli*. It is a fact that after colonization, conquerors begin to see the indigenous culture as either cute or quaint. These accounts of emperors being acclaimed by a conquered race may not be so impeccable. In Roman eyes, female oracles were exotic, relating back to the ancient classical oracles like the Delphi sibyl. But the fact remains that several of the reported oracles of the Celtic world were female.

Let us witness a séance in action. When Queen Medbh of Connacht visits Fedelm, a *banfáith* or seeress, in the story of the Cattle Raid of Cooley, *Táin Bó Cuailgne*, she specifically enquires whether she has the *Imbas Forosna*, or 'the kindling of inspiration' before she asks her question; and in order to strengthen her luck, her charioteer first turns Medbh's chariot *deiseal,* or sunwise. In her own chariot, Fedelm sits with three plaits of hair down her back, clothed in a variegated cloak, carrying a weaver's beam of white bronze, while each eye sports the three pupils of vision:

> Medbh asked the maiden, 'What is your name?' 'Fedelm, poetess of Connacht,' she replied. 'From whence do you come?' asked Medbh. 'From Albion, having learned the art of divination,' answered the

maiden. 'Have you the power of prophecy called *Imbas Forosna*?' 'Indeed I have,' said the maiden. 'Then look for me and tell me how my hosting will fare.' As the maiden looked, Medbh said: 'O Prophetess Fedelm, what is the fate of the army?' Fedelm replied: 'I see it bloody, I see it red.' 'That cannot be so,' said Medbh, 'for Conchobor lies under the weakness of the *noinend* in Emain together with the Ulstermen and all the mightiest of their warriors, so my messengers have reported to me. O Prophetess Fedelm, how do you see our host?' Medbh asked again. 'I see it stained with blood, I see it red,' said the maiden. 'Not so,' said Medb, 'for Celtchar mac Uthidir has joined at Dún Lethglaise together with a third of the men of Ulster, and Fergus mac Roeich meic Echdach is exiled with us with his three thousand men. O Prophetess Fedelm, how do you see our host?' 'I see it blood-stained, I see it red,' answered the maiden. 'Well, no matter,' said Medbh, 'for in every hosting and army encamped together there are always quarrels and conflict and bloody woundings. Look once more for us, and tell us the truth. O Prophetess, how do you see our host?' 'I see it blood-stained, I see it red,' said Fedelm and she spoke as follows:

'I see a fair man who will perform weapon-feats, with many wounds upon his flesh. On his brow, the hero light shines. His forehead is the assembly of many virtues. Seven jewel-bright, heroic pupils shine in each of his eyes. He has unsheathed his spearpoints. He wears a red mantle with clasps. His beautiful face attracts women. This handsome youth looks in the battle like a dragon. His powers are like those of Cú Chulainn of Murthemne, and though I do not know this famous Cú Chulainn, I do know that he will give bloody wounds to the army. I see a tall man in the plain who gives battle to the host. He holds four small swords in each hand to perform great deeds. He attacks with his *gáe bolga* [belly spear] and with his ivory-hilted sword and his spear. He can employ them on the host. Each of his casting weapons has its own special use. This man wrapped in a red mantle sets his foot on every battle-field. He attacks his foes across the left wheel-rim of his chariot. The distorted one kills them. I see that he has changed from the form in which hitherto he has appeared to me. He has moved forward to the battle. Unless you take warning, there will be destruction. I think that it is Cú Chulainn mac Súaldaim who comes against you. He will kill your entire army. He will slaughter you in dense crowds. A thousand severed heads will be heaped about him. Fedelm the prophetess does not conceal your fate. Blood will flow from heroes' bodies. The hand of this

> hero will wreak great harm. He will kill warriors; the
> men of Clan Dedad mac Sin will flee. Men's bodies
> will be hacked and women will weep because of the
> Smith's Hound whom I now see.'[3]

From her repeated questioning of the seeress and her gainsaying the results, we immediately understand the impatient nature of Queen Medbh. We also note that Fedelm reports the future in the present tense, as if she is clearly envisioning Cú Chulainn's spirited defence of Ulster against Medbh's troops before her. The weaver's beam in her hand, reminds us that Fedelm is a servant of the weavers of fate, yet, in the face of this most devastating prophecy, Medbh continues her hosting against Ulster regardless.

The commonest druidic prophecies relate to the moments of conception and of death, giving seers a premonitory power that inspired great fear or respect. When the druid of Druim Díl was consulted by King Eoghan of Munster, he realized from the king's horoscope that Eoghan would be imminently killed in battle, but that a son conceived on that very night might become a powerful king. The druid sent his daughter Moncha to sleep with Eoghan, who died the very next day. Moncha grew pregnant but, as her term approached, she had to prevent the birth from occurring before the correct planetary conjunction, so she sat upon a stone as she bore down. Her child's name, Fiachu Muilleathan (Flathead), tells us how the delay manifested![4]

The premonition of impending death is one of the most prevailing evidences of seership, but seers are notoriously chary in speaking about it, as we see from St Adomnan's *Vita Columbae*, where a young nobleman, Gore, asks Columcille how he shall die. Using the veiled language of seership, the saint replies: 'You will die neither in battle, nor in the sea. A companion of your journey will be the cause of your death.' When pressed to be more specific, Columcille refuses to say more, so that he will not burden Gore's mind with the knowledge, lest he become overly anxious. Some years later, Gore was whittling with his knife when he had to rise to part some fighting men. In the altercation, Gore stumbled against his own knife and suddenly remembered the prophecy. He died, not of his relatively minor wound, but out of anxiety of mind at the foretold words.[5]

Those who ask about themselves seldom hear good news. Macbeth is a good example of one who becomes prophecy's victim. Hailed by the Weird Sisters as Thane of Glamis, Thane of Cawdor, and as King Hereafter, he not only believes the words but also 'helps' them to come true. On his second meeting with the Sisters, they conjure spirits who tell him the second part of the prophecy: to beware the Thane of Fife (Macduff), that none of woman born shall kill him, that he cannot be vanquished till Birnam Wood comes to Dunsinane. His final disillusionment is voiced in:

And be these juggling fiends no more believ'd

That palter with us in a double sense,

That keep the word of promise to our ear

And break it to our hope!

Just as poets were recognized by their skill with the Three Illuminations, so it seems that the druids were famed by their ability to prophesy the triple death. The druid Bécc mac Dé, prophesied that the 6th-century King of Tara, Diarmuid mac Cerbaill, would be killed by Aéd Dubh mac Suibhni Araidi, so prince Aéd was banished from Ireland. In addition, St Rúadán had also cursed Tara, saying that a rooftree (ridgepole) would fall upon Diarmuid. In such a welter of prophecies about his death, Diarmuid mac Cerbaill inquired of his druids how he would die. 'By slaughter,' said the first, 'you will be wearing a shirt grown from a single flax-seed with a mantle of one sheep's wool on the night of your death.' The second druid said, 'By drowning: the ale brewed from one grain of corn shall kill you.' The third said, 'By burning; the bacon of a pig that never was farrowed shall be on your dish that night.'

On his circuit, Diarmuid travelled right-hand-wise round Ireland from Tara into Leinster, Munster, Connacht, Ulster, so that he would arrive at Tara in time for his Samhain office. On circuit, the warrior Banbhán invited him to spend a night as his guest. Diarmuid's wife, Mughain, refused, for she felt it was ill omened. Banbhán greeted Diarmuid, giving him his own beautiful young foster daughter to be the king's wife. While they waited for dinner, Banbhán asked the woman if she'd brought a garment for the king: she produced a shirt made of one flax seed that had miraculously become a field full; also a mantle made of one sheep's wool.

While they dined, Banbhán proclaimed the excellently flavoured bacon had never been farrowed, but that the piglets in question had been of Caesarean delivery. The ale, also, had been brewed from a single grain of corn found in the crop of a ringdove. Diarmuid then looked up and saw that the lower part of the house was new, but that the roof was old. Banbhán explained that once they had seen the ridge-beam of a house floating on the sea, which they had retrieved and stuck on his own house. Then Diarmuid realized that Bécc mac Dé's prophecy was coming true and that Banbhán was none other than Aédh. As Diarmuid rose to leave, Aéd flung a spear through the king's chest so that his spine was broken. As Diarmuid fell back into the house, the hosts of Ulster descended upon the house and set it alight. To hide from the flames, the king dived into the ale-vat as the rooftree finally broke and fell upon him.[6] Prophecy is a sure way of cutting kings down to size, but here Diarmuid dies the ancient threefold death of the kingly sacrifice by drowning, burning and hanging, as foretold by both druids and a Christian cleric!

The triple-death theme reappears in the medieval *Vita Merlini* where Ganeida brings a young man to her brother,

Merlin, who prophesies his death by falling from a rock. She brings the boy in again, disguised, and is told by Merlin that the boy will meet a violent death in a tree. The boy comes back disguised as a girl, and Merlin prophesies a death in a river. Everyone laughs, but later, the boy grows up to die in a freak accident while out hunting; he falls from a height, his foot catches in a tree, submerging his head in a river – thus neatly fulfilling all of Merlin's prophecies.[7]

Similarly, in the *Life of St Kentigern* we hear how the wild man, Lailoken, hails Kentigern while he is celebrating an open-air mass and demands the sacrament so that 'he can pass into blessedness'. Kentigern asks what death Lailoken will die, and if he will die that day. Lailoken then prophesies his own triple death: that he will be stoned and clubbed; that he will be pierced by a stake; that he will be drowned. Each of these death prophecies is told to Kentigern via an intermediary, and disbelieved as mere ravings. Finally, Lailoken bewails his fate and begs Kentigern to come to him with the sacrament that will be his viaticum. As Kentigern approaches, Lailoken climbs down from his rock and is given what he desires, with the proviso that 'whoever is worthy to receive this sacrament will live for ever and will not die, but whoever receives it unworthily will die wholly and will not live'. Lailoken then rushes off. Later that day he is stoned and beaten by shepherds of King Meldred; at the moment of his death he falls down the bank of the River Tweed, is pierced by a sharp stake in a fish pool and drowns. In these stories of the triple death, we see a working out of the oath of the elements: all three elements break the mortal body and liberate the soul back to the three worlds.

Druidic prophecy often provides ambiguous and seemingly impossible conditions that inculcate either uncaring or cautious behaviour in the one who dares to ask after his fate: forever after, he must live looking over his shoulder or peering anxiously ahead, as it says in the story of Fingen's Nightwatch:

> Whatever wonders you say will come to me,
>
> It seems to bode me no good to
>   hear the druid's lay.[8]

Prophecy and the Signs of the Times

The border between madness and inspiration is sometimes hard to distinguish by those who look upon an entranced prophet. The doubtful outcome of prophecy is often mirrored in the dangerous process of becoming a vision poet. On the summit of the impressive mountain, Cadair Idris (The Chair of Idris) in northwest Wales, is a rocky hollow resembling a couch. Traditionally, anyone passing a night there would be rendered either dead or mad, or else become a poet. The early Victorian poet Felicia D Hemans wrote, as if held in the sway of that experience:

I lay there in silence – a spirit came o'er me;
   Man's tongue hath no language to speak what
   I saw:
Things glorious, unearthly, pass'd floating
   before me,
And my heart almost fainted with rapture and awe.
I view'd the dread beings around us that hover,
   Though veil'd by the mists of mortality's breath;
And I call'd upon darkness the vision to cover,
   For a strife was within me of madness
   and death.[9]

What a prophet sees cannot be put back in the box or ignored; it can be an experience whose contemplation brings mental derangement or despair. Then there is responsibility, for imparting prophecy can be too heavy for one. True prophets are not popular, as the prophet Jonah knew well: in the Book of Jonah he sails to Tarsish or Tartessos by the Pillars of Hercules, rather than deliver the prophecy of the Creator in person to the city of Ninevah where death might await him.[10] We have already seen how Coinnech Odhar tried to fend off the inconvenient question whose truthful answer led to his death (p.11). How dangerous is it to be a prophet?

For the young Myrddin Emrys it is nearly fatal, until he uses his prophetic skills in such a virtuoso manner that all thought of his death is cancelled. When the usurping British

King Vortigern's tower keeps falling down, his druids prescribe the blood of 'a boy with no father' as human cement. Vortigern's men find a boy whose mother was said to have slept with a spirit, but when the young Myrddin, whom we know better as Merlin, is brought to be sacrificed, he demands to know what is causing the tower to fall down: when the druids cannot tell him, Merlin tells them:

> 'Drain the pool and at the bottom you will see two hollow stones, and in them two dragons asleep.' The king … found as Merlin had said; and now was possessed with the greatest admiration of him. Nor were the rest that were present less amazed at his wisdom, thinking it to be no less than divine inspiration.[11]

A white and a red dragon immediately emerge and begin to fight, upon which Vortigern asks what this means. On hearing this question, Merlin bursts into tears, falls into a trance and utters his prophecies concerning the land of Britain. Geoffrey of Monmouth's 12th-century *Historia Regum Britanniae* is the earliest account of the prophecies of Merlin; many relate to subsequent rulers or the battles between the British and the Saxons, while others are clearly of more recent times. 'The monks in their cowls shall be forced to marry, and their cry shall be heard upon the mountains of the Alps', seems to relate to the Reformation of England, while 'the sea over which men sail to Gaul shall be contracted into a narrow channel' references the Channel Tunnel. 'At that time shall the stones speak, and the sea towards the Gallic coast be contracted into a narrow space. On each bank shall one man hear another' suggests quartz technology, the internet and mobile phones.[12] Further prophecies relate to a time when the constellations move out of their paths.

Myrddin Emrys (Ambrosius) of the prophecies is a different character from that of Myrddin Wyllt (the Wild) who runs mad after witnessing the horrors of war, yet Geoffrey of Monmouth fuses both beings together as Merlin, who is both wise and deranged, the herald of the Pendragon's reign.

Later versions of Merlin's prophecies were published all over Europe, as his name was used to authenticate and give authority to later prophecies that were the stuff of popular almanacs. Another prophet who has enjoyed a similar fame, and to whom many subsequent prophecies have been imputed, is Thomas of Ercildoune. He lived in the 13th century and is the eponymous hero Thomas the Rhymer of the Scottish ballad, who was given 'the tongue that would never lie' by the Queen of Faerie, upon whose lap he lay. This gift of second sight did not endear him to all in his circle. The Earl of Buchan thought little of Thomas' prophetic gift and went about calling him 'Thomas the Liar', to which the seer responded:

> Thomas the Liar thou callest me,
> But a sooth [true] tale I shall tell to thee.

> By Aikyside thy horse shall ride,
> He shall stumble and thou shalt fa'.
> They neck-bane shall break in twa,
> And dogs shall thy banes gnaw,
> And maugre [despite] all thy kin and thee,
> Thy own belt thy bier shall be.[13]

Indeed, on Aiky Brae in Aberdeenshire, the earl was thrown from his horse and killed outright. Thomas also prophesied the catastrophic death of King Alexander III of Scotland in 1286, telling the Earl of March, the previous day, that at the next noon 'such a tempest should blow as Scotland had not felt for many years before'. Since the next day was clear and no apparent change in the weather predicted, the earl scorned Thomas as an impostor. But no sooner were the words out of his mouth than a messenger arrived to report the king's death: he had fallen from his horse over the cliff at what is now Kinghorn, in Fife. He left Scotland without an heir, wide open to English incursion. The Countess of Dunbar is said to have asked Thomas when the terrible Scottish–English wars would end. His riddling reply tells her:

> When people have made a king
>   of a capped man …
> When hares litter on the hearthstone …
> When Bambourne [Bannockburn]

> is dunged with dead men ...
> When shall this be? Neither in
> thy time nor in mine;
> But [shall] come and go within
> twenty winters and one.[14]

The 'capped man' is a fool, and has been taken as a reference to Edward II's disastrous reign; while Bannockburn in 1314 was the Scottish victory that paved the way to a return to Scotland's independence ten years later.

The use of questions to provoke prophetic answers is found in the words of Gerald of Wales who speaks of the *awenyddion* or 'inspired ones':

> Among the Welsh there are certain individuals called *awenyddion* ... When you consult them about some problem, they immediately go into a trance and lose control of their senses, as if they are possessed. They do not answer the question put to them in any logical way. Words stream from their mouths, incoherently, and apparently meaningless and without any sense at all, but all the same well expressed; and if you listen carefully to what they say you will receive the solution to your problem ... When it is all over, they will recover from their trance, as if they were ordinary people waking from a heavy sleep, but you have to give them a good

shake before they regain control of themselves … They seem to receive this gift of divination through visions, which they see in their dreams. Some of them have the impression that honey or sugary milk is being smeared on their mouths; others say that a sheet of paper with words written on it is pressed against their lips.[15]

Gerald of Wales was in the invidious position of being employed by the Normans, the very race that had conquered his own people. His almost schizophrenic account veers between native pride in the skill of the *awenyddion* and clerical disdain for an oral, indigenous oracle that doesn't use logic or writing. That he has obviously interviewed these prophets is clear, because the impressions of 'honey or sugary milk' on their mouths seem too detailed to be invented. This rare account is one of the earliest references to a prophetic tradition parallel to the Irish *Three Illuminations*.

Sometimes the voice of prophecy speaks, not from a human seer, but directly from the gods to our world as an oracle. Since the turn of the third millennium, prophecies of Armageddon, cosmological meltdown and the end of the world have plied their doom-laden trade, creating considerable anxiety and anguish. It is worth remembering that the pre-Christian Celtic tradition had no sense of the world's beginning nor of its ending. It is not until visions of Celtic saints that the endings and punishments prefigured in the biblical Book of Revelation find fresh exposition.

In the Second Battle of Mag Tuiread, it is the battle goddess, Morrighan, who proclaims the victory of the Tuatha de Danaan over the Fomorians to the mountains and rivers. She speaks peace to the land in words of blessing:

> Peace high as heaven, Heaven to the earth,
>   Earth under heaven, Strength in everyone.
>
> Cup's great fullness, Fullness of honey,
>   Mead till satiety, Summer in winter.
>
> Spear reliant on shield, Shield reliant on
>   host, Host upon occasion for battle.
>
> Grazing for sheep, Wood grown like
>   antlers, Weapons forever departing,
>
> Mast upon the trees, Boughs low
>   bending, Bending with increase.
>
> Wealth for a son, A son strong-necked; Yoke
>   of a bull, A bull from a praise song.
>
> Refrain for a tree, Wood for a fire, Fire
>   for the asking, Rock from the soil,
>
> Woven into victories; Boyne for hostel,
>   Hostel of resonant extent.
>
> Green growth after spring, Autumn increase
>   of horses, A company for the land, Land
>   with trade to its furthest shore; May it be
>   mighty-forested, perpetually-sovereign!
>
> Peace high as heaven, Life eternally.[16]

The Morrighan, who we must remember is the goddess of carrion when in her crow form, also prophesies the signs of an alternative world-order:

> I shall not see a world Which will be dear to me:
>
> Summer without blossoms, Cattle
>   will be without milk,
>
> Women without modesty, Men without valour.
>
> Conquests without a king …
>   Woods without mast.
>
> Sea without produce … False
>   judgements of old men.
>
> False precedents of lawyers, Every man
>   a betrayer. Every son a reaver.
>
> The son will go to the bed of his father, The
>   father will go to the bed of his son.
>
> Each his brother's brother-in-law. Nobody
>   will seek a woman outside his house …
>
> An evil time. Son will deceive his father.
>   Daughter will deceive her mother …[17]

Such portents of disordered nature are the traditional signposts of the prophet to come, and point the way back to the ancestral restorative of thankfulness and offering, as Merlin reminds in his prayer on regaining his sanity once again:

Therefore, highest Creator, I should be obedient to thee, that I may show forth Thy most worthy praise from a worthy heart, always joyfully making joyful offerings. For twice Thy generous hand has benefited me alone, in giving me the gift of this new fountain out of the green grass. For now I have the water which hitherto I lacked, and by drinking of it my brains have been made whole. But whence comes this virtue, O dear companion, that this new fountain breaks out thus, and makes me myself again who up to now was as though insane and beside myself? [18]

When human anxiety and trouble overwhelm us, the truth is hard to seek. But instead of ploughing on till the last day of doom, in fulfilment of horrific, world-ending prophecies, we can turn back and look once more into the treasury of our destiny. The gifts that have been given to us not only look forward to the future, but also back to their roots in the past. Ancestral memory preserves the way of right behaviour, if we would only live according to the way of truth:

> Let him preserve justice, for so
>   it will preserve him …
> Let him exalt mercy and it will
>   truly exalt him …
> Let him observe the driver of an old chariot.
> For the driver of an old chariot does not sleep:

He looks ahead, behind, in front
   and to the right and left;

he looks out, he defends, he protects,
   so that he may not break

by neglect or violence the wheel-rims
   which run under him …

It is through the justice of the ruler
   that each great man of art attains
   the diadem of knowledge.[19]

This instruction is from the *Fir Flathemon* or 'The Prince's Truth,' a tract for rulers. Like the chariot-driver, a prophet stands in a place of truthful vigilance, seeing with the eyes of the past as much as the eyes of the future. The circularity of prophetic vision shows the connection between cause and effect, but no prophecy is fixed or inevitable, for in the end:

Darkness yields to light,
   Sorrow yields to joy.

A churl yields to a wiseman,
   A serf yields to a freeman.

Meanness yields to generosity.
   Anarchy yields to proper rule,

Conflict yields to peace,
   Falsehood yields to truth.[20]

Questioning the Universe

The deepest prophecies are announced in dreams and heralded by our questions. Without your question, the universe cannot respond. But can you live with the answer that your question brings? In seeking after truth, fashion your question well; ensure it asks what you mean. Questions that result in yes/no answers give insufficient information, while conditional questions that ask 'should' have already unseated you. Stand in a place of responsibility, ask worthily and respectfully, never trivially. At dawn or twilight, sit with your question and utter it into the space of truth that you have made between your two hands. Your question, like a stone sinking into a pool, sends its ripples throughout the two sides of reality. Like a prayer, it must travel until it is met somewhere in the universe, so do not expect an instant response. The answer may be felt as a vibration or deep physical knowing while you are about your day, or in dreams, in the unsuspecting mouth of someone who speaks to you, in the newspaper you are reading that week, as a letter you receive next month. When response comes, hold it tenderly as a bird that has flown into your hands for a moment, give thanks for having received it, letting it flow into your three cauldrons. You are now a vessel of truth: speak the truth that you have received and act upon it.

CHAPTER 8

Omens and Divination

*Taliesin the bard, son of Don … had great
foresight through the interpretation of portents:
with wondrous eloquence, he proclaimed in
prophetic utterances the lucky and unlucky lives
of lucky and unlucky men.*

'De Sancto Iudicaelo Rege Historia'

Classical Celtic Divination

The word 'divination' derives from 'to ask the gods'. Not all seers used divination, although many had their own signs and idiosyncratic associated meanings; some employed ancient methods that survive into our own times. Some divined by dreams, cloud-shapes, the running or flight of animals. Divination uses the widest variety of criteria to determine guidance, from the omens of nature and the movement of birds, to complex systems of discernment that rely upon the fall of sticks, stones and other matters. Indeed, one can divine from whatever is in the universe.

In Iron Age Celtic Britain, as yet uncolonized by Romans, divination was the professional preserve of the *ofyddion*, the vates (or ovates) while, in Ireland, seers were called *faithí,* but some important divination fell to rulers, as when the Icenian Queen Boudicca made an augury before battle. She released a hare from a fold of her robe and watched its track. It ran in the auspicious direction and Boudicca thanked the goddess Andrasta (the Invincible One), saying:

> I call out to you as one woman to another, imploring and praying to you for victory, and for the maintenance of life and freedom against arrogant, unjust, insatiable and profane men.[1]

The hare obviously ran the successful way, since Boudicca went on to lead a smashing assault upon the Roman colonial towns of Verulamium, Londinium and Camulodunum.

There may have been portable divining devices also. Across Britain and Ireland, 10 pairs of bronze Iron Age spoons have been found, believed to be part of the druidic divination equipment: they date from the same period and have a distinctive appearance. Shaped like a pointed tea-caddy spoon, with a short handle that could only have been held between finger and thumb, one of a pair has an equal-armed cross engraved on it, creating four quarters, while the other is plain with a tiny hole drilled on one side near the edge. Another pair, dated from 50BC to AD100, was found in a bog near Crosby Ravensworth, Westmorland. The engraved spoon has a central circle where the quartered sections meet, creating a possible fivefold field of divination, which recalls the sacred fivefold divisions of Ireland. The Penbryn Spoons from Ceredigion in Wales have a distinguishing feature that is not present in the others. The quartered spoon has inlaid dots of different metals – gold, silver and copper in its quarters. It is possible that other sets of spoons may have lost their inlaid dots, of course, or that there were different modes of divination.

Archaeologists speculate that some substance is poured through the hole of the plain spoon so that it lands in the quartered spoon, creating some kind of divinatory pattern that can be interpreted, depending on what and where it forms.

It is suggested that a powder was used.[2] Substances that lend themselves to divination would be oil or a semi-liquid such as runny honey, both of which would form patterns or trails in water. The manner in which the liquid landed upon the lower quartered spoon would be random enough to create a series of possible divinations. Experiment has proved that oil runs better, whereas water can hardly be made to pass through the very small hole where it merely makes a viscous bubble over it.

Another suggestion by Cat Hooley-Jones is that the spoons may have been placed over the eyes, to create darkness, as was the custom for poets in the houses of darkness. In support of this, one pair of spoons from Upper Walmer was found with one spoon either side of the skull.[3]

Hydromancy, or divining by liquid, was used by the *baru* or diviner priests of Mesopotamia, who used to pour oil into a bowl of water: if the bowl were of translucent alabaster, the patterns of the divinatory substance would have shone in sunlight or torchlight:

> Some poured clear water into a bowl or a cup and then strewed into the water small pieces or particles of gold and of silver or even of precious stones. Some poured oil into the water. Still others observed the manner in which light rays broke on the surface. Usually the resulting designs to be observed in the water, whether from the particles thrown into it or

from the oil, were construed after certain rules in order to draw conclusions as to the future.[4]

In Genesis, Joseph uses this same method of hydromancy, when he purposely places his silver cup in the sack of his departing brother, Benjamin. Sending his steward after him, he bids him accuse Benjamin with the following words: 'Is this not the cup from which my lord drinks and in which he divines?' [5] Methods of hydromantic cup divination were common in the Middle East and may have influenced the Persian myth of Jamshid's Cup, the *jam jehan nima*, or 'cup showing the universe', which may lead us to consider the spoons in a different way.

The four-way division of the bronze spoon with its inlaid metallic dots is strangely reminiscent of an island in the Voyage of Maelduin, an 8th-century *immram* or voyage text, where the hero and his men visit 32 island locations in the Western Atlantic.

> The next island had four fences dividing it; the four enclosures were like this: a golden one with kings inside; a silver one with queens inside; a brass one with warriors inside; a crystal one with maidens inside. A maiden brought hospitality and, from the little vessel she served them from, they lay drunken for three days.[6]

These four divisions of the island are not only fenced by the four precious substances, but they each contain a different visionary being. The gold, silver and copper dots found upon the Penbryn spoons may represent the luminaries of the sun, the moon and the stars, with the fourth representing the earth.

The Auspicious Day

Alongside the methods of the professional seers, there have always existed commonplace ways of understanding the omens, auguries and portents of everyday life. Some omens come bidden, while some are unbidden and have significance within a particular community because they are familial signs, such as hearing the *beansí*'s wailing as a death portent. Other signs are not significant in themselves unless they precede a planned journey or expedition, or unless they are seen in response to a question or issue that is held in the heart and mind of the seer.

St Columcille made a Christian refutation of all druidic omens in this verse, which references both bird omens and *ogam* (*see* Glossary, *ogham*), as well as other portents for which we have no information.

> Our destiny does not lie with the sneeze
> Nor with the bird at the top of the bough,
> Nor with the trunk of a knotty tree,
>   Nor with the humming drone.
> I do not venerate the voice of the bird,

Nor the sneeze, nor the destiny
of the earthly world,
Nor a son, nor luck, nor a woman;
Christ the Son of God is my druid.[7]

The way people sneezed was obviously an omen, and then, as now, people obviously judged their luck by their relationships or children. The act of humming may have indicated the mode in which some seers searched for things, or it may have been a divination by the chance tune that people sing as they go about.

Across the world, many people will not embark on any important enterprise, whether it be a long voyage, a business contract or a marriage, without first seeking the most auspicious day. Astrologers are often consulted to determine such days. In the ancient Celtic world, the one consulted would have been the druid. In the Ulster Cycle, we hear how Nessa consults the druid Cathbad to determine what the day is good for. He tells her that it's a good day to beget a king upon a queen. She promptly sleeps with him and they conceive Conchobor mac Nessa, who becomes king of Ulster. Similarly, Cathbad is consulted by the young boy, Setanta, who asks what the day is good for: he is told that it is auspicious for 'taking valour' or the arms of manhood, and that the boy who takes arms on that day will be the most famous hero of Ireland, although his life will be short. Setanta promptly demands arms of his foster-father and grows up to become the hero Cúchulainn.

The Coligny Calendar, a 1st-century AD Gaulish calendar, which runs over a five-year period, shows that it was composed by a series of observations of the night sky over many years. Auspicious days are marked MAT (good) while inauspicious ones are called ANM(AT) (not good).

This tradition continued into Christian times, although the omens of the days were influenced by the Christian calendar: in the Scottish Highlands, Sunday was a good day to be born, but a day without permissible work. Monday was unlucky for finishing the harvest. Tuesday was good for cutting grain or sharpening a blade. Wednesday was considered lucky for many enterprises. Friday was not a day on which to count flocks and herds. No cutting, shearing, reaping or hair-cutting happened on this day, though one might plant and sow. Formal betrothals happened on Fridays. Saturday was not a day for debt-collection or borrowing. Thursday, the day of St Columcille, was propitious for many kinds of work, as we see:

> Thursday of gentle Columcille,
>   Day to put sheep to fatten,
> Day to get a cow with calf,
>   Day to set up the loom,
> Day to put a coracle on the sea,
>   Day to put valour in a banner,
> Day to give birth, day to day,
>   Day to hunt upon the heights.

> Day to harness horses,
>> Day to take herds to pasture,
> Day to make earnest prayer,
>> Day of my beloved is Thursday.[8]

In Brittany and in Wales, the 12 days of Christmas, which mark the intercalary days of the year, are called the Omen Days. Each of the 12 days is assigned to a month of the coming year, with the first day of Christmas symbolic of January, the second day of February etc. The omens experienced on each of the Omen Days indicate the nature of each month in the coming year.

Observation of the star cycles helped to reveal the destiny of those who were about to be born. Maithghean, the druid who owned the slave Broiseach, mother of St Brighid, divined from the sound of the chariot in which the pregnant slave was brought to him, that her child was going to be a marvellous being. As Broiseach brought milk into the druid's house at sunrise, she had one foot on either side of the threshold as she gave birth, denoting that her daughter would have 'one foot in either world'.[9]

Common Divinations

In default of professional seers and diviners, people made their own divinatory forms: some are simple, like the *crois-tàradh* whereby anyone can pull a stick out of a hedge and divine, and others are full of complex lore like the *slinneachadh* which reads the marks upon bone.

The *crois-tàradh* or 'cross-measure' is a method of receiving a yes/no response. The instruction was simply to 'take a chance stick and measure it in thumb-breadths, beginning at its thick or lower end, and saying, when the thumb is laid on the stick, no or yes.'[10] Alternating yes or no, in this way, the last thumb measure gives the answer. This is supported from an earlier 17th-century manuscript in the Bodleian Library, which speaks of the Highland practice: 'in suddein Danger, they cleav a staf, & put (pull) a stick off it, burning it a little, which they send from hand to hand.' [11] 'Sending it from hand to hand' reveals how the *crois-tàradh* was done, with the stick held in front of the operator as the opposing thumb widths are taken. *Crois-tàradh* may be a descendant of *crandchur* or 'wood setting', a taking of lots from slips of wood.

Slinneanachd (Scots Gaelic) is scapulimancy or divining from a sheep's shoulder-blade. Widespread in the Gaelic world, it has been utilized all over the world since the first domestication of animals. The complete criteria for the Gaelic form of divining was not recorded, although we have both Arabic and medieval Latin diagrams relating what each part of the scapula is good for. This lore was obviously adapted to local regions where the art was used. In the 18th century, John Ramsay of Ochertyre, specified that only the scapula of black, one-year-old sheep be used, and it was important that the moon shouldn't change between the sheep's death and the scapula's use. He knew that distinct parts of the scapula were assigned to the clans living in the region, so that omens could be read in accordance with one's neighbours' fortunes. The scapula had to be prepared by boiling off the flesh and could not be touched either by teeth or knife. Writing in the 12th century about immigrant Flemings in Pembrokeshire, Gerald of Wales relates that their scapulimancy shows:

> most confidently from signs of certain little cracks and
> marks the symptoms of approaching peace and war,
> murders and fire, adulteries in the house, the fortune
> of the king, his life and death.[12]

The two sides of the scapula were read differently: the inside of the shoulder-blade, where the spine protrudes, related to the private events of the household, while the outer side denoted public events. Only close members of the family read the inner side, since any notable marks would connect intimately to them.

The ogam lists in the Book of Ballymote give Son Ogam or *Macogam* as a means of divining the sex of an unborn child. If it is the pregnant woman's first child, the letters in her name are reckoned up: if the count is even, the child will be a girl; if odd, then it will be a boy. If the woman has existing children, the last child's name is reckoned up. This seems a pathetically unsatisfactory divinatory method compared to the rich allusive kennings of ogam available to the *fili*.

This oracle from a 17th-century Irish manuscript, *The Book of the O'Connor Don,* uses chance-met travellers' names as an oracle:

> The first person you meet when you are bound on a journey, ask his name, if you don't know it. If A, O, U, E, I are the first letter of his name, you will be lucky and come home safely. If B, C, D, then joy will be in your coming and going. If P or Q or T, the love of a woman is signified. If F, L, M, N, R, or S, you will not come safely home nor succeed beneficially. If it be X, Y, Z, that means immediate death or loss of your goods on the journey.[13]

Neladoracht was the art of cloud divination. In the story of The Siege of Druim Damgaire, the Druid of Dáithí is reported to go to the top of Cnoc nan Druad in Sligo on the feast of Samhain, and remain there until sunrise, in order to foretell from the clouds.[14] *Néladoir* or 'cloud diviner' is the Irish name that was used in the Middle Ages for an astrologer.

The use of a wisp of straw seems to have originated with the druids, who would often enchant a wisp and send it on the spirit wind to anyone whom they would send mad. A 17th-century seer from Colonsay in the Hebrides used the oracle of the three straw crosses, assisted by her familiar spirit, to see what lay beyond human sight. When asking a question of her spirit, she had to lay the straw crosses on the palm of her hand. When she did so:

a great ugly Beast sprang out of the earth near her
and flew in the air. If what she enquired had success
according to her wish, the Beast would descend calmly
and lick up the crosses. If it would not succeed, the
Beast would furiously thrust her and the crosses over
the ground, and so vanish to his place.[15]

The furious beast of this oracle might well be a poetic kenning
for the wind, which has its own powers.

'Shoe casting' was a form of divination, known from the
inauguration rituals of the Scottish kings. The 'casting', or
throwing of a single shoe, was done over a newly inaugurated
king by the king's caster, presumably to see what kind of reign
he would give.[16] At their inauguration, early Gaelic kings literally stepped into the footstep of the ancestor, graven into a rock
like the one at Dunadd in Argyll. The nature of shoe casting
becomes clearer to us if we examine a poem composed by the
14th-century Scottish poet, O Mail Chairáin, on the occasion
of a divination he had made to see if his absent son, Ferchar,
was still alive.

> I threw a shoe over a house
> Speaking the bright red-haired one's name;
> A man ran across to see
> If it had landed top under sole.[17]

From this context, we see that the landing of the upright shoe would mean that the poet's son was still alive and that if it landed upside down, with the sole uppermost, then it would betoken death.

Augury of the Frith

Finding lost things and people has been a central and very real skill of seers, whose visions enabled lost objects, drowned bodies, lost children or stray animals to be found. We have an example of the discovery of a thief from the *Vita Columbae*, the Life of Saint Columcille, abbot of Iona. He called upon two of his brothers to go seek a poor thief called Erc, whose location he had precisely envisioned by means of his augury or *frith*:

> Now cross the strait to the island of Mull, and look for the thief Erc, in the little plains beside the sea. He came last night secretly, alone, from the isle of Coll, and he is trying to conceal himself during the day among sand-hills, under his boat, which he has covered with grass; so that by night he may sail across to the small island where the sea-calves [seals] that belong to us breed and are bred; in order that the greedy robber may fill his boat with those that he thievishly kills, and make his way back to his dwelling.[18]

The monks find and detain Erc but, because the thief is starving, Columcille sends him home with a gift of mutton instead of the seal-meat he intended to take.

The *frith* is a Scots Gaelic method of augury, or seeking out information by means of the observation of signs in nature. The Scottish name Freer is an anglicization of the title *Frithir* or Augurer. Members of the Frithir family were hereditary augurers of the kings of Scotland in the Middle Ages. The *frith* was undertaken for many purposes: to ascertain the nature of the season ahead, to find what was lost, to ask a question and to receive an omen about a planned enterprise.

The *frith* was done on the first Monday of the quarter; quarter days were the equinoxes and solstices of the year when the rent was due, but in earlier times, the *frith* was probably done on the quarter days of the Celtic year – Samhain, Imbolc, Beltane and Lughnasa. Domestic beasts were locked up, so that they shouldn't become inadvertent objects of the *frith*. Fasting and barefoot, bare-headed and with closed eyes, standing at sunrise, at the doorsill, facing outward with a hand on each jamb, the *frithir* spoke the augury invocation and opened his eyes. Whatever the eyes lighted upon gave the augury or divinatory sign of the season.

> Some say that while doing so, he walks sunwise around the fire, which is in the middle of the floor of the house, and that he walks thrice around it, once

in the name of the Father, once in the name of the Son, once in the name of the Holy Spirit … He then goes with closed or blindfolded eyes to the door step of the house, and places a hand on each jamb. He appeals again to the all-seeing God to grant him his request. He opens his eyes, and looking steadfastly before him, without moving his eyes or his eyelids to right or to the left, upward or down, he carefully notes all that he beholds. According to some, he crosses the threshold and goes sunwise around his house, keeping his gaze always before him as described, and saying or chanting the hymn. From the nature and position of objects within his sight, he draws his conclusions.[19]

As with many Celtic rituals, it was proper to invoke spiritual help before making the *frith*:

> God over me, God under me,
>> God before me, God behind me,
>
> Myself upon your path,
>> God, Thou, God, in my steps.
>
> The frith made by Mary to her Son,
>> The offering of Bride through her hollow hands,
>
> Saw you it, O King of Nature? –
>> Said the King of Nature that he saw.
>
> The augury of Mary for her own child,
>> Early made during his circuit,

> Knowledge of truth rather than knowledge of lies,
>> That I myself may see my word's vision.
>
> Son of Fair Mary, King of Nature,
>> Give me vision of my own word,
>
> With unfailing grace, in the asssembly,
>> That shall never be quenched or diminished. [20]

This invocation remembers the incident when the young Jesus' guardians lost him when they went up to Jerusalem. In Gaelic tradition, St Brighid (Bride) was said to be the foster-mother of Jesus, and she and Mary, his mother, are often invoked as the guardians of this augury, since they were the first to do it to find Jesus. The *frith* is sometimes also known as the Augury of Mary or of the Well, or of Bride.

The *frith* requires a viewing frame, which demarcates the area in which it is done. We've seen that a doorway facing the outside was used, remarkably like the linteled doorway of dolmens, but a free-standing style was also possible by making a tube or telescope of the hands together. This made a path between the worlds to the place of quietness and vision:

> The frith that Brighid made for her Fosterling,
>> Making a pipe within her palms:
>
> 'I see my Fosterling by the well-side,
>> Teaching the people without doubt.'[21]

The *frith* prayer was spoken through the tube to clear the way and may hark back to the poetic method of *Imbas Forosna* (p.94), which also uses the palms of the hands, as we can see by these two extracts from the 'Augury of Brighid':

> The augury made by Mary for her Son,
>> Breathed by Brighid through her palm;
>
> Have you seen the frith, O Guiding Maid?
>> Said the Guiding Maid, she had.[22]

It may be thought that such portents are the result of coincidence, but the ability to read the book of nature is dependent upon the formation of an issue or question, a focusing of intent. Until that moment, the signs in nature are insignificant; but once the intent and search for an answer have begun, nature becomes charged with meaning and is a book that we can always read.

Not all omens have the same weight. *Manadh* is a prophetic omen of some gravity, while *meanmhain* (little signs) and *sgrìob* (twitches) are portents that come as infinitesimal sensations, or apprehensions that are physically experienced by one or more of the senses. These physical signs are well known: a rising or lowering of temperature, a crawling of the skin, a raising of the hair, the sudden overshadowing of an emotion or mood that has no immediate cause, a sinking sensation in the pit of the stomach, a trembling or shaking, or else bursting into tears or being drenched in sweat. We commonly experience all these physical signs when we perceive something unseen, though we seldom note or remember these signs. In this *manadh*, collected in the Western Isles in the 19th century, we also see that the fasting seer takes a sitting, bent-over position to prepare for his augury, which he is in the act of repeating: what he sees are not fortunate omens:

> Early one Monday morning,
>   I heard the lamb's bleating,
> And the goat-bleat of snipe,
>   While sitting bent in augury,
> And the grey-blue cuckoo,
>   And with no food within me.
>
> At Tuesday evening's close, I saw
>   on the smooth stone
> The pale, slimy snail,
>   And the white wheatear
> On the top of the stony dyke,
>   The foal of the old mare,
> Club-footed, its back turned to me,
>   And I discerned from these signs
> That the year would not go well with me.[23]

The omens of the *frith* vary from place to place: some are *sealbhach* (lucky) or *rosadach* (unfortunate). The following list of some of the Gaelic omens gives us an idea of the lucky and unlucky portents that the *frithir* might encounter. Here are some of the *sealbhach* or fortunate signs:

> A man coming toward you. An excellent sign.
>
> A cock looking toward you.
>   Also an excellent sign.
>
> A man standing is a sign of a sick man
>   recovering and casting off illness.
>
> A beast rising up – a sign of a man
>   recovering and throwing off illness.
>
> A bird on the wing – a good sign.
>
> A bird on the wing coming to you
>   – sign of a letter coming.
>
> A woman seen passing or
>   returning – not so bad.
>
> A woman with brown hair – luckiest.
>
> A lark – a good sign.
>
> A dove – a good sign.
>
> A wild duck – a good sign.
>
> A dog – good luck.
>
> A cat – good for Mackintoshes only.
>   To others it is considered *rosadach*.
>   The cat is regarded as evil, as
>   shown by the fact that witches are
>   believed to assume this form.

> A pig – good for Campbells. For
>   others indifferent when facing you;
>   bad with its back toward you.
>
> A calf or lamb – lucky with its face
>   to you; good showing its side.
>
> A horse – lucky.
>
> A brown horse is the best.[24]

Some of these signs are helpful to certain clans but not to others, as with the cat that appears in the Mackintosh clan badge as descendants of Clan Chattan, Clan of the Cat, while a boar's head is the crest of Clan Campbell. Here are some of the *rosadach* or unlucky signs:

> A man lying down means sickness
>   or continued illness.
>
> A beast lying down augurs sickness,
>   continued illness or death.
>
> A woman seen standing – a bad sign, such
>   as death, or some untoward event.
>
> A woman with red hair – not lucky.
>
> A woman with fair hair – not lucky.
>
> A woman with black hair – lucky.
>
> Fowls without a cock in their
>   midst – not a good sign.
>
> Stonechat – untoward.

A crow or raven – a bad sign; death.

A sparrow – not lucky, but blessed. It
foretells the death of a child.

A chestnut or red horse – a bad sign; death.[25]

Many omens are lucky because of their association with the Holy Family in some way; ducks were considered blessed because of a tradition that when Jesus had to take refuge overnight in a heap of straw, hens scraped it away and exposed him, but ducks pushed it back again.[26] On the other hand, red hair was universally unlucky as an omen, especially on a red-haired woman, because Judas Iscariot was traditionally thought to be red-headed. The Highland saying, 'A man should cross himself should he see a woman when making the *frith*', is typical of the fear of women's supernatural power.[27] Such fear is found in the earliest *loricas* or protection prayers, where protection is sought against 'the spells of women, smiths and druids'.[28]

The calls, movements and presence of birds have a central place in the Celtic lore of omens. As we have seen from the *frith*, movements of birds gave their own oracles. *Historia Britonum*, an ancient Irish poem, speaks of six druids who lived at Breagh-magh, practising 'the watching of birds'.[29]

The Irish cleric, Augustinus Hibernicus, writing about the existence of miracles after the sixth day of creation, said the transformation of one thing into another 'animal to tree, bread to stone, man to bird' was against the law of God and nature.

To hold otherwise was 'to give assent to the laughable tales told by the druids, who say that their forebears flew through the ages in the form of birds'.[30] Such bird lore is still scattered throughout Britain and Ireland today. When a bird comes significantly near to a house, or comes inside through a window, many people will take this as an omen of death; few remember the cause of this belief, but the visiting bird is believed to be an ancestor who is coming to take one of the household away.

Eugene O'Curry transcribed a Middle Irish account of divination by bird calls. The sounds of the raven also betoken words that are appropriate to the guest expected:

> If the raven call from above an enclosed bed in the midst of the house, it is a distinguished grey-haired guest or clerics that are coming to thee, but there is a difference between them: if it be a lay cleric the raven says *bacach* [stick-holder]; if it be a man in orders, it calls *gradh gradh* [love] and twice in the day it calls. If it be warrior guests or satirists that are coming it is *gracc gracc* [beloved] it calls, or *grob grob* [frown], and it calls in the quarter behind thee, and it is thence that the guests are coming. If it call *gracc gracc* the warriors are oppressed- [?] to whom it calls. If women are coming it calls long. If it call from the north-east end of the house, robbers are about to steal the horses. If it call from the house door, strangers or soldiers

are coming. If it call from above the door, satirists or guests from a king's retinue are coming. If it call from above the goodman's bed, the place where his weapons will be, and he going on a journey, he will not come back safe; but if not, he will come back sound. If it is the woman who is about to die, it is from the pillow it calls. If it call from the foot of the man's bed, his son or his brother or his son-in-law will come to the house. If it call from the edge of the storehouse where the food is kept, there will be increase of food from the quarter it calls, that is, flesh-meat or first milking of kine. If its face be between the storehouse and the fire, agreeable guests are coming to the house. If it be near to the woman of the house, where her seat is, the guests are for her, namely, a son-in-law or a friend. If it call from the south of the storehouse, fosterage or guests from afar are coming to the house. If it speak with a small voice, that is, *err err* or *úr úr*, sickness will fall on someone in the house or on some of the cattle. If wolves are coming among the sheep, it is from the sheep-fold it calls, or from over against the good woman, and what it says is *carna carna* [flesh], *groh grob* [croak], *coin coin* [wolves]. If it call from the roof-tree of the house when people are eating, they throw away that food. If it call from a stone, it is death-tidings of an *aithech* [churl]. If it call

from a high tree, then it is death-tidings of a young
lord. If from the top of the tree, death-tidings of a
king or a youth of noble lineage. If it go with thee on
a journey or in front of thee, and if it be joyful, thy
journey will prosper and fresh meat will be given to
thee. If thou come left-hand-wise and it calls before
thee, he is a doomed man on whom it calls thus, or
it is the wounding of some one of the company. If it
be before thee when going to an assembly, there will
be an uprising therein. If it be left-hand-wise it has
come, some one is slain in that uprising. If it call from
the corner where the horses are, robbers are about to
attack them. If it turn on its back thereat and says *grob
grob*, some of the horses will be stolen and they will
not be recovered, and so on.[31]

The wren, the king of all birds, had its own divinatory lore. As
with the raven, the directions from which the wren calls is also
significant. The lore of the directions is very much influenced
by the direction from which the many-coloured winds blow.[32]

If the little white-headed one call to thee from the
east, pious men are journeying towards thee, with
discourtesy for thee. If the wren call from the south-
east, it is proud jesters that are coming. If from the
south-west, ex-freemen [slaves] are coming to you.
If it call from the north-east, folk with a bedfellow or

women are coming. If it be from the north, dear to thee is he that is coming. If it come from the northwest, pious folk are on the way. If it call from the south side of thee, provided it be not between thee and the sun, a fond visitation is coming to you. If it be between thee and the sun, it is the slaying of a man that is dear to thee, or a horn on thyself. If it be at thy left ear, union with a young man from afar, or sleeping with a young woman. If it call from behind thee, importuning of thy wife by another man in despite of thee. If it be on the ground behind thee, thy wife will be taken from thee by force. If the wren call from the east, poets are coming toward thee, or tidings from them. If it call behind thee from the south, thou wilt see the heads of good clergy, or hear death-tidings of noble ex-laymen. If it call from the south-west, robbers and evil rustics and bad women are coming toward thee. If it be from the west, wicked kinsmen are coming. If it call from the north-west, a noble hero of good lineage and noble hospitallers and good women are coming. If it call from the north, bad people are coming, whether warriors or clerics or bad women, and wicked youths are on the way. If it call from the south, sickness or wolves among thy herds. If it be from the ground or from a stone or from a cross it calls, death-tidings of a great man it relates to thee. If it call from many crosses, it is a slaughter of men, and the number of times it alights on the ground is the number of dead it announces, and the quarter toward which its face is, from thence are the dead it announces.[33]

Birds come as messengers of visitors, losses, fortune, sickness and death, once well known to the vision-seers. But while professional divination remained the preserve of the Irish *filí* right through the Middle Ages, nearly everywhere else many of these methods lapsed into folk divinations that everyone could practise, becoming a mixture of Christian prayers and half-remembered lore. These ancestral omens can live again as we take note of the living creatures that surround us. They are the living reminders that stitch the two sides of reality together, whereby the relationship between everyday vision and other-worldly vision can be discerned.

Finding Omens For Your Frith

The old omen lists of our ancestors are largely fragmentary, or have little relevance to modern life, where in towns we may be unlikely to observe chickens or deer on a daily basis. But wherever we are in the world, there are signs that you can still read. The way to learn your own omens is by the act of making a *frith* daily and also noting which birds, animals, weather conditions etc. are speaking clearly to you. For example, I've learned that, where I live, the appearance of a wagtail usually denotes extremely cold weather or even snow. Rather than relying on a list of omens from another culture, it is best to see the whole of nature as a book, and to note, at the time of your *frith*, what you understand at that time, without psychology, rationalization or guesswork. First, make an intent or question, such as 'Please show me the resources of this day': without a well-framed question whatever you experience will be merely random information. Secondly, make your own prayer to see and understand the truth. Then stand outside, before eating breakfast, and with the question in your heart, with eyes closed. Turn yourself round, stop and then open your eyes. Note *the first thing* that you experience when you look ahead: movement of birds, sounds, cloud-shapes, a piece of rubbish in the gutter – these might all be auguries for you. Note also your feelings, your memories, and what is invoked from within your own understanding, rather than 'looking up' what things denote. Daily repetition and checking of your *frith* will give you insights into the *gléfiosa*, the bright knowledge that is your heritage.

CHAPTER 9

Visions of Wholeness

*There are some ... on whom divine favour has
bestowed the gift of contemplating, clearly and
very distinctly, with scope of mind miraculously
enlarged, in one and the same moment,
as though under one ray of the sun, ever the
whole circle of the whole earth, with the
ocean and sky about it.*

St Adomnan, *Vita Columbae*

Oath of the Elements

One of the key features of our age is the keen loss of a vision of wholeness. In the Celtic vision, the ability to hold both the visible and invisible halves of reality in one vision, brought a measure of wholeness, not only to those who had this grace, but also to those who heard these stories and poems of wholeness spoken aloud. This vision of honouring 'all that is' has attracted many people to the Celtic tradition, which saw no division between the seen and unseen worlds. That there can be a way of perceiving and holding all life in one equal measure of respect is now the challenge for us today.

It is easy to fall into a 'golden age of the Celts' rapture when regarding the ancestral ability to perceive and rhapsodize about nature, but this is only one side of the picture. We must set beside it the elemental oath, which was a core precept of all Celtic nations. The Gaulish version of the oath was: 'If I break faith with you, may the skies fall upon me, may the seas drown me, may the earth rise up and swallow me.'

We see the remains of this oath in the words of Myrddin, who ran into the Caledon Forest in the grip of battle fatigue. So severe was the loss of his comrades that:

> Since the battle of Arfderydd I have
>   been unmoved by everything,
> Even though the sky were to fall
>   or the sea to overflow.[1]

In the story of Culhwch and Olwen, Arthur himself swears to his nephew:

> I will grant whatever your tongue may name, as far as wind dries, rain wets, sun revolves and sea encircles and earth extends.[2]

To swear by the elements was no hollow promise, as we see from the fate of Laegaire MacNeill, King of Tara in the time of St Patrick. While attempting to exact tribute from the Leinstermen, Laegaire became their prisoner. His release was incumbent upon the usual guarantees of good behaviour, for which he swore by 'sun and moon, water and air, day and night, sea and land, to never again demand tribute'. The violation of his oath, when he invaded Leinster to claim the tribute two years later, was precisely answered, for 'the sun and wind killed him because he had violated them'. As the 12th-century manuscript, *Book of the Dun Cow*, says, 'no one dared violate the elements at that time'.[3]

The 1st-century BC Greek historian, Diodorus Siculus, said of the druids that they 'joined to the study of nature that of moral philosophy, asserting that the human soul is indestructible, and also the universe, but that some time or other, fire and water will prevail'.[4]

The *Book of Leinster* gives us the full substance of this primordial oath, where King Conchobor bids the servants of his household to take his place in the battle line against the

Connachta, while he goes north to check out who is attacking him on the northern border. They swear as follows:

> We shall do so, for heaven is above us and earth beneath us and the sea all around us, and unless the firmament with its showers of stars fall upon the surface of the earth, or unless the blue-bordered, fish-abounding sea come over the face of the world, or unless the earth quake … we shall never retreat one inch from this spot until such time as you return.[5]

What does this tell us? That for the ancient Celts, there were not four elements, but three – the air from the sky, water from the sea, and earth from the land. The implicit fourth element of fire resided in the sun, in the hearth-fire, in the sacred fires of Brighid, the goddess of inspiration. The three primordial elements are also associated with the three worlds that make up the universe: the sky of the upper world, the earth of the middle world and the waters of the lower world.

The sky above, the earth on which life was lived and the sea beneath, were the air, earth and water that sustained life: worthy witnesses of good behaviour indeed, but only in a world that respected the elements. We live in a world no different from our ancestors, except that we now have the ability to disrupt the order of the elements forever by the skill of our hands. We are pressed into a narrow place as environmental pollution and the collapse of the natural order stare us in the face. Even the

Christian Celts did not so wantonly ignore the elemental powers, giving the title of 'King of the Elements' to Christ, so that the ancient elemental respect was upheld. What was at the heart of the Celt's elemental respect? What was at the heart of their vision of wholeness?

Sources of Inspiration

Myths of the sources of inspired wisdom interweave the traditions of Ireland and Britain. The Irish *imbas* and the British *awen* were the words for 'inspiration'. A vision of wholeness depended upon the interchange between this world and the other. Inspiration was seen to flow into our world out of the otherworld, so that it was only by making this bridge that wholeness could be maintained. As we've already seen, the chief architects of that bridge were the *aosdana*, 'the people of the gift', whose poetry, visions and prophecies were the fruit of that union between the worlds.

In Ireland, the location of the source of inspiration was believed to be the mythic Well of Segais or the Well of Conla, a spring which was believed to be the source of the Boyne and Shannon rivers, although they have separate origins. Both the stories below come from the Irish metrical *dindsenchas*, which are topological myths explaining the origins of the name and underlying story of a place. Two stories are told concerning the origin of these rivers, both relating to divine ancestors and matrons of inspiration.

The myth of Boann, wife of Nechtan, relates how Nechtan had a secret well from which flowed powerful waters:

> None could look in the well's depths,
>> But his two bright eyes would burst;
> And if he dared moved to left or right,
>> Then he would not come away without a wound.
>
> So it was that no-one dared approach it,
>> Except Nechtain and his cupbearers,
> Famous for their brilliant deed,
>> Flesc, Lam and Luam.
>
> One day, white Boann came here,
>> To dare these powers for herself.
> As she walked three times round the well,
>> Three waves burst from it, causing her death.
>
> Each wave struck against limb,
>> Disfiguring the soft-blooming woman;
> A wave against her foot, a wave against her eye
>> A third wave shattered one hand.[6]

Boann effectively loses one side of her body, in a way reminiscent of the *corrguineacht* posture, which cancels one side of the body (*see* p.123). In this instance, Boann's daring act of not only looking into it but also moving three times around it, releases the power of the River Boyne from the spring, as a force of benefit to all, while short-circuiting its power through her own body. A similar story is told of the source of the Shannon.

Shannon, or Sinann, in its Middle Irish version here, is a maiden who similarly goes to gaze upon the well of Segais and drowns in its waters. We are told that many rivers arise from the well, but only the Shannon is renowned. It reveals the heart of the myth, which all vision poets held dear:

> Here you will find the magic lore of Segais
>   excellently, under the true spring:
> over the well of the mighty waters stands the
>   poets' music-haunted hazel.
>
> Connla's well, loud its music, lay beneath the
>   blue-rimmed ocean:
> six streams, unequal in fame, rise from it, the
>   seventh was Sinann.
>
> The nine hazels of Crimall the sage drop their
>   nuts into the well:
> they grow there by the power of magic spells
>   under a mysterious mist of druidry.
>
> Together grow, in extraordinary ways,
>   with leaves and with their flowers:

a wonder is this, though a noble quality,
   wonderously ripening all at once.

When the cluster of nuts is ripe, they fall down
   into the well:

they scatter below on the bottom, and the
   salmon eat them.[7]

From this myth it is clear that the well is within the boundaries of the otherworld, since it is beneath the sea in the land of Tir Fa Thon or 'Land Under Wave'. We also learn that the salmon of knowledge, who swims in the waters of the Well of Segais, is attracted there by nine hazel trees which are in blossom, bud and nut at the same time. Whoever catches and eats of the salmon of knowledge becomes wise beyond the measure of men.

The motif of the woman who uncovers the well is a myth found all over the Celtic world and forms the nearest we have to a Celtic creation myth. Instead of letting water pool in one place, Boann and Sinann's action creates a river of wisdom from which many can drink. Memory of primeval inundation remained deeply embedded in Celtic consciousness. Some catastrophic and creative primordial event provided the basis for most of the myths of inspirational origin: a motif that associated wisdom with water's overflowing, whether it be from a well, a sea-dyke or from a cauldron, as we see from the Breton legend of Ker Ys, to the Welsh legend of the drowned lands of Gwyddno

Garanhir (Gwyddno Tall Crane), father of Elffin, patron of the poet Taliesin. It was a poetic precept that inspiration was to be found at the edge of the sea.[8]

The quest for the source of inspiration is at the heart of two myths, central to Celtic story. When Fionn mac Cumhail was living under his boyhood name of Demne, he was set to become a poet, not a warrior. He served his teacher Finneces (White Wisdom), who had been seeking for the salmon of wisdom for seven years, since it had been prophesied. Finally, the salmon is caught and Demne is commanded to prepare it for eating. Unfortunately for Finneces, the salmon-juice spurts out and lands on Demne's thumb, which he then thrusts into his mouth in order to cool it. As an Irish folk tale relates it:

> To ease the pain, [Demne] put it between his teeth
> and gnawed the skin to the flesh, the flesh to the bone,
> the bone to the marrow, and when he had tasted the
> marrow, he received the knowledge of all things.[9]

Finneces graciously acknowledges that the salmon must have truly been intended for his pupil, and forever afterwards Demne/Fionn is granted the knowledge he seeks by the simple act of chewing upon his thumb.

A similar story of the theft of wisdom is given in *Ystoria Taliesin*, a late Welsh folktale that has its roots firmly in the ancient mythic bedrock. It tells how Gwion was set to tend the fire of Ceridwen, who was brewing up a year's worth of ingredients to create an inspirational brew, to enhance the gifts of her ugly son, Afagddu. Again, Gwion receives the three drops of inspiration from the cauldron as it bubbles up, and it is he who is imbued with the gift as he sucks his fingers. Being omniscient, he now understands that Ceridwen is furious and he hides in a sequence of animal shapes, which are chased by Ceridwen, who shapeshifts into the predator of each animal as they chase through the elements of earth, water, air and fire: hare and greyhound, fish and otter, bird and falcon; until Gwion hides as a grain of wheat in a heap of wheat and Ceridwen becomes a red hen who scrabbles him up. Finally, Gwion is reborn of Ceridwen and cast in a leather bag upon the waters.

He fetches up in a salmon weir when the disconsolate youth, Elffin, son of Gwyddno, has been promised the catch of the weir that night. As he unhooks the bag and opens it, the baby within tells him not to be dismayed. Elffin names the child with his first words – 'What a radiant brow!' – and the reborn Gwion becomes the infant poet, Taliesin.[10]

As when a tincture has been poured into two vessels, we recognize the original myth, although the vessels have taken individual colourations. The two legends of Fionn and Taliesin find their counterpoint in each other: Demne sucks up the hot salmon juices, while Gwion drinks the cauldron's inspirational drops; Demne eats the salmon of knowledge, while Taliesin becomes the salmon. The lands of Elffin's father, Gwyddno, are drowned because of the overspilling of the cauldron of Ceridwen, for once the three knowledge-bearing drops fly out onto Gwion's fingers, the rest of the contents are poisonous. Thus, the rest of the cauldron's brew poisons the horses of Gwyddno. If we read 'horses' as a poetic kenning for the sea, then we have a potential link between the Irish well-uncovering myth and the Welsh cauldron myth.

Another link between the two myths is the number nine. Nine is the luckiest of numbers, being the multiple 3 x 3; three itself is the prime number among the Celts. 'The number Three is sacred with them … next to that Nine. When any thing succeeds not for three times, they try it nine times, and then give it over.'[11] Wisdom was remembered in triads by druids and poets on both sides of the Irish Sea. In Ireland, it is the nine hazel trees of the Well of Segais that provide the nuts that fall into the waters to be eaten by the salmon of knowledge. In Wales, it is the nine maidens who dwell at the heart of the underworldly realm of *Annwfyn*, the In-world; they blow their breath over the pearl- and enamel-rimmed cauldron of the underworld, heating it with inspiration. It is not hard to envisage the spirits of the nine hazels as nine slender women of the otherworld, whose wisdom inspires the wise in our world.

Only by going into the otherworld can the treasure of inspiration be gained, as we see in the 9th-century Welsh poem *Preiddeu Annwfyn*, the Raiding of the Underworld, when Arthur quests for the Lord of the Underworld's cauldron. Taliesin returns to the sea, from which he was drawn by Elffin, this time on board Arthur's ship *Prydwen* in order to sail into the depths of Annwfyn. Amid the seven caers or towers of that difficult place, Taliesin sings of his *awen*:

> My original song stems from the cauldron,
>
> By the breath of nine maidens was it kindled.
>
> The Chief of Annwfyn's cauldron,
>> what is its power?
>
> Ridged with enamel, rimmed with pearl,
>
> It will not boil the coward's portion,
>> it is not destined.[12]

The hero's portion, the *curadmír* was the cut given to the bravest of warriors at the feast. It came out of the cauldron, itself a poetic kenning for the sea. By communion with the otherworld, by the deeds of our hands, by the fulfilment of our ancestral gifts, we all aspire to manifest the potential within us.

The Celtic vision understands all human beings to be completely made up of the universal elements, where man is not separate from nature, as we can see from the 10th-century Irish Saltair na Rann:

> It is worth knowing that Adam was made of eight parts: the first part of earth; the second part of sea; the third part of sun; the fourth part of clouds; the fifth part of wind; the sixth part of stones; the seventh part

of the Holy Ghost, [the eighth part of the light of the world]. The part of the earth is the man's body; the part of the sea is the man's blood; the part of the sun is his face and his appearance; [*the part of the clouds is omitted*]; the part of the wind, the man's breath; the part of the stones, his bones; the part of the Holy Ghost, his soul; the part that was made of the Light of the World is his piety. If earthiness is prevalent in the man, he will be slothful. If it be the sea, he will be changeful. If it be the sun, he will be beautiful, lively. If it be the clouds, he will be light, foolish. If it be the wind, he will be strong to every one. If it be the stones, he will be hard to subdue, a greedy thief. If it be the Holy Ghost, he will be lively, of a good appearance, and be full of the grace of the divine scripture. If it be the light, he will be a loveable, sensible man.[13]

Within the Saltair's theology is wound a more ancient under-standing, that is uttered most clearly by the 9th-century Irish theologian, Johns Scottus Erigena, giving us the true nature of the Celtic vision of wholeness:

In man is established every visible and invisible creature. Therefore he is called the workshop of all things, because in him are contained all things subsequent to God. And hence it comes about that he is called the midpoint. For he comprehends in himself and brings into one, extremes far removed from one another: the spiritual and corporeal realms. For he consists of body and soul.[14]

This Neo-Platonic Christian understanding is echoed within the Reverend Robert Kirk's account of the faeries' beliefs:

For 'tis one of their Tenets, That nothing perisheth, but (as the Sun and Year) everie thing goes in a Circle, Lesser or Greater, and is renewed and refreshed in its revolutions, as 'tis another, That Every Body in the Creation, moves, (Which is a sort of Life:) and that nothing moves but what has another Animall moving on it, and so on, to the utmost minutest corpuscle that's capable to be a receptacle of Lyfe.[15]

Kirk's words convey not only 17th-century interest in the physiological workings of the human body (possibly influenced from the early atomic work of Robert Boyle), but are redolent of a more native understanding of the interconnectedness of all life, the sense of which is growing ever stronger. How can we regain this sense of wholeness and interconnectedness through the medium of seership and vision?

The Workshop of All Things

The possibility of reassembling our understanding, or bringing soul and body into one place, is extended to us in Geoffrey of Monmouth's account of the derangement of Merlin. Traumatized by the horrors of the Battle of Arfderydd where he sees his kinfolk slain, Merlin runs maddened into the Forest of Caledon and hides for several seasons. Many well-meaning attempts are made to bring him back to civilized society, which he rebuffs, and it is only when his friend, the poet Taliesin, comes to sit quietly with him that healing is possible. After a long sojourn in the wilds, in all weathers, Merlin asks a question so seemingly trivial that we might miss its importance. He asks Taliesin, 'Why does rain arise?'

Taliesin, under the guidance of Minerva (or Brigantia), answers by relating the creation of the world from the elements; he speaks of the waters and the air, and all the animals who inhabit them, giving an account of the history of Britain and how he and Merlin conducted Arthur's body into Avalon, and many other matters. While the creation of the world, as related to Merlin by Taliesin, owes more to Isidore of Seville than to Welsh native lore, it does demonstrate the healing power of telling the story of 'all that is', so that those who have lost the place in their own story might be restored to it. No sooner has Taliesin completed his account when a spring bursts forth and Merlin drinks from it, and is restored to himself.

He turned his face toward the stars and uttered devout words of praise. 'O King, through whom the machine of the starry heavens exists, through whom the sea and the land with its pleasing grass give forth and nourish their offspring and with their profuse fertility give frequent aid to mankind, through whom sense has returned and the error of my mind has vanished! I was carried away from myself and like a spirit I knew the acts of past peoples and predicted the future. Then, since I knew the secrets of things and the flight of birds and the wandering motions of the stars and the gliding of the fishes, all this vexed me and denied a natural rest to my human mind by a severe law. Now I have come to myself and I seem to be moved with a vigour such as was wont to animate my limbs.[16]

Other madmen and derelicts come to drink from the spring, and Merlin recognizes his old friend Maeldinus among them. With the voice of personal experience, Merlin says to him:

Now that you have recovered your reason, do not shun the bushes or the green glades that you inhabited while you were mad, but stay with me that you may strive to make up in service to God for the days that the force of madness took from you. From now on all things shall be in common between you and me in this service, so long as either lives.[17]

Together with Taliesin and Merlin's sister, Ganeida, they aim to live secluded in nature, so that there might be no distraction from the vision of wholeness that they have attained. Merlin retires and leaves the work of prophecy to his sister, upon whom the vision falls, for there must always be someone who speaks for the people. As Taliesin's poem 'Hostile Confederacy' relates:

> I know the law of fertile inspiration
> when it is skilful, to those happy days,
> to a quiet life, to the defence of the times,
> to kings who bestow consolation,
> to all who are on the face of the earth.[18]

Despite the delusion that we live solely within the world of the senses, despite the disdain in which the spiritual transactive skills of seership and vision are held, the dialogue between our world and the other continues, the two edges of reality sewn together into one fabric by those who perceptions and understandings show them the truth of life. Even within the skewed, disjointed times in which we live, the seer's duty still is to see for the community, to envision and remember wholeness, to bridge the two halves of reality, so that life is made holy again. May that vision ever endure!

The Bright Knowledge

The mind's limits being miraculously loosed, they clearly and most plainly behold the whole of the earth, together with the circuit of the oceans and the heavens, in one single moment, as if beneath a single ray of the sun.

Vita Columbae I. 43

To kindle the bright knowledge, visit a source of living water: a well, a spring, a lake, a river or the sea. Understand the waters as a pathway that bridges the everyday world and the otherworld. Do you dare to seek the source of inspiration? Then listen to what the waters say, look within their depths. What stories and myths arise from this place? Even though you are ignorant of local lore, listen to the waters. When you close your eyes, what images arise, what songs shimmer? To what source in the otherworld do the waters lead? Only by following the stories will you find the source.

In the darkness, kindle a flame or lay a fire, and gaze into the heart of the light. As you strike the match, be aware of the stored energy that is about to ignite the dry materials of wick, wood or paper into conflagration. Consider, what is tinder dry within you that awaits the flame? What kindles into light at the approach of inspiration? What myths and stories are your stories, too? What teachings shimmer in the fire's gleads?

The *gléfiosa* does not arrive from passive contemplation, it is kindled when you are cooked. It is knowledge that burns you, scalds your soul, makes you twist inside your skin until you are able to accommodate its proximity. It always wants to be in circulation, dancing on the tip of your tongue or the toes of your feet, sparkling from the ends of your fingers, beaming from your brow or shooting out of the top of your head. It spirals in and out of you all the time, but only if you are faithful to the vision of wholeness that it brings. The moment that you think you've fixed knowledge down, or have become wise, that is the moment when it departs from you, for it will not inhabit the house of the dead.

May the blessing of the *gléfiosa* dwell within you as a gift that you give to others, as a gift that you forever receive at the edge of inspiration.

Chapter Notes

Below, CM indicates my own translation. General classical or biblical references are not in the bibliography but can be consulted easily online.

Chapter 1 – Seers, Healers and Prophets

[1] Ellis, Peter Berresford, *The Druids,* (Constable, London, 1994), p.66

[2] Ellis, *The Druids*, p.64

[3] *Diogenes Laertius, Vitae, I.5*

[4] *Lebor Gabala Erenn* (5 vols), trans. R.A. Stewart MacAlister, (Irish Texts Society, Dublin, 1938–56)

[5] Matthews, Caitlín, *Elements of Celtic Tradition*, (Element, Shaftesbury, 1989), p.47

[6] CM

[7] Koch, John T. & John Carey eds., *The Celtic Heroic Age: Literary Souces for Ancient Celtic Europe and Early Ireland and Wales,* (Celtic Studies, Malden, 1995), p.50

[8] Wilby, Emma, *Cunning Folk and Familiar Spirits*, (Sussex Academic Press, Brighton, 2005)

[9] Davidson, Hilda Ellis ed., *The Seer in Celtic and Other Traditions* (John Donaldson, Edinburgh, 1989), p.28

[10] Sutherland, Elizabeth *Ravens and Black Rain* (Constable, London, 1985), p.200

[11] Innes, Christian, *The Brahan Seer Trail,* (Highland News Group, 2001), p.8

[12] ibid.

[13] ibid.

[14] Sutherland, *Ravens and Black Rain*, p.204

[15] Sutherland, *Ravens and Black Rain*, p.205

[16] Campbell, John Gregorson, *Witchcraft and Second Sight in the Highlands and Islands of Scotland*, (James MacLehose, Glasgow, 1902), p.274

[17] ibid.

[18] ibid.

[19] Hunter, Michael ed. *The Occult Laboratory: Magic, Science and Second Sight in Late 17th-Century Scotland,* (Boydell Press, Woodbridge, 2001), p.111

[20] Matthews, Caitlín & John *Encyclopedia of Celtic Wisdom: A Celtic Shaman's Sourcebook,* (Element Books, Shaftesbury, 1994), p.297

[21] personal relation of Dwina Murphy Gibb

[22] MacKenzie, William, *Gaelic Incantations, Charms and Blessings of the Hebrides*, (Transactions of the Gaelic Society of Inverness, 1895)

[23] Davidson, *The Seer in Celtic and Other Traditions*, p.28

Chapter 2 – Seeing the Invisible

[1] Martin, Martin, *A Description of the Western Isles of Scotland.* http://www.appins.org/martin.htm

[2] ibid.

[3] Davidson, *The Seer in Celtic and Other Traditions*, p.1

[4] Martin, *A Description of the Western Isles of Scotland*

[5] Stewart, R.J. *Robert Kirk: Walker Between Worlds*, (Element Books, Shaftesbury, 1990), p.33

[6] Martin, *A Description of the Western Isles of Scotland*

[7] Stewart, *Robert Kirk: Walker Between Worlds*, p.33

[8] Murray. James A. ed. *The Romance and Prophecies of Thomas of Erceldoune,* (Early English Text Society, London, 1875), p.11

[9] Wilby, *Cunning Folk and Familiar Spirits*, p.69

[10] Ellis, *The Druids*, p.223

[11] Spence, Lewis, *Second Sight: Its History and Origins*, (Rider, London, 1951), p.31

[12] Matthews, Caitlín & John, *Celtic Myth and Legend,* (Folio Society, London, 2007)

[13] Kirk, Robert, ed. Stewart Sanderson, *The Secret Common-Wealth*, (D.S. Brewer, Cambridge, 1976)

[14] Matthews, John, *Taliesin: Shamanism and the Bardic Mysteries in Britain and Ireland,* (Aquarian, London, 1991)

[15] Martin, *A Description of the Western Isles of Scotland*

[16] traditional English folk song

[17] CM

[18] O'Curry, Eugene, *On the Manners and Customs of the Ancient Irish*, (Williams and Norgate, Dublin, 1873), vol 2

[19] Koch, *The Celtic Heroic Age,* pp.387–9

[20] Carey, John, *King of Mysteries: Early Irish Religious Writings*, (Four Courts, Press, Dublin, 2000), pp.201–2

[21] Davidson, *The Seer in Celtic and Other Traditions*, p.18

Chapter 3 –Faery Seership

[1] Dooley, Ann & Harry Roe, *Tales of the Elders of Ireland*, (Oxford University Press, Oxford, 1999), p.5

[2] Kirk, *The Secret Common-Wealth*, p.80

[3] *Medieval folklore: an Encyclopedia of Myths, Legends, Tales, Beliefs, and Customs* ed. Carl Lindahl, John McNamara, John Lindow, (Oxford University Press, Oxford, 2002), p.190, CM trans.

[4] Dooley, *Tales of the Elders of Ireland,* p.51

[5] Gregory, Lady Augusta, *Visions and Beliefs in the West of Ireland,* (Colin Smythe Ltd. Gerrards Cross, 1977)

[6] Martin: *A Description of the Western Isles of Scotland*

[7] Henderson, Lizanne & Edward J. Cowan, *Scottish Fairy Belief,* (Tuckwell Press, Phantassie, 2001), p.84, CM trans.

[8] Campbell, *Witchcraft and Second Sight in the Highlands and Islands of Scotland*, p.141

[9] Stewart, *Robert Kirk: Walker Between Worlds,* p.29

[10] Wilby, *Cunning Folk and Familiar Spirits*, p.95

[11] Martin

[12] CM

[13] Matthews, C. & J. *Encyclopedia of Celtic Wisdom: A Celtic Shaman's Sourcebook*

[14] Carmichael, Alexander, *Ortha nan Gaidheal*, (6 vols, Oliver & Boyd, Edinburgh, 1971), vol 2, pp.255–6

[15] Henderson, *Scottish Fairy Belief,* p.125

[16] Geoffrey of Monmouth, *Vita Merlini*, trans. J.J. Parry, http://www.sacred-texts.com/neu/eng/vm/vmeng.htm

[17] Davidson, *The Seer in Celtic and Other Traditions*, p.15

[18] Sharkey, John, *The Medicine Tree: Traditional Healing in Wales from Pre-History to the Present,* (Llanerch Press, Cribyn, 2008), p.109

[19] Stewart, *Robert Kirk: Walker Between Worlds,* p.23

[20] ibid.

[21] ibid.

[22] Wilby, *Cunning Folk and Familiar Spirits*, p.xi

[23] Stewart, *Robert Kirk: Walker Between Worlds*, p.60

[24] Wilby, *Cunning Folk and Familiar Spirits*, p.36 English modernized CM.

[25] ibid. p.97

[26] ibid. p.56

[27] Matthews, C. & J., *Encyclopedia of Celtic Wisdom: A Celtic Shaman's Sourcebook*, p.410

[28] Rees, Alwyn & Brinley, *Celtic Heritage*, (Thames & Hudson, London, 1971), pp.200–01

[29] Matthews, Caitlín, *The Celtic Book of the Dead*, (Connections, London, 1992)

[30] Matthews, Caitlín, *King Arthur's Raid on the Underworld*, (Gothic Image, Glastonbury, 2008)

[31] Davies, Sioned, *The Mabinogion,* (Oxford University Press, Oxford, 2007)

[32] Matthews, C., *The Celtic Book of the Dead*

[33] Matthews, C.& J., *Celtic Myth and Legend*

Chapter 4 – Vision Poets

[1] Matthews, J. *Taliesin: Shamanism and the Bardic Mysteries in Britain and Ireland*

[2] Matthews, C. & J., *Celtic Myth and Legend*

[3] Strabo, *Geographies*, IV, 4, c.197, 41.

[4] Neat, Timothy with John MacInnes, *Living Poets and Ancient Tradition in the Highlands and Islands of Scotland,* (Canongate, Edinburgh, 1999), p.338

[5] Finlay, Ian, *Columba*, (Richard Drew Publishing Ltd., Glasgow, 1979), p.158

[6] Neat, *The Voice of the Bard*, p.324

[7] Julius Caesar, *De Bello Gallico*, 6:1.

[8] Meyer, Kuno trans. *Selections from Ancient Irish Poetry*, Constable & Co. Ltd., London, 1913

[9] Carey, *King of Mysteries: Early Irish Religious Writings*, p.31

[10] Corkery, Daniel, *The Hidden Ireland*, (Gill and Macmillan, Dublin, 1967)

[11] Martin, *A Description of the Western Isles*

[12] Hunter, *The Occult Laboratory*

[13] Corkery, *The Hidden Ireland*, p.88

[14] Matthews, C., *King Arthur's Raid on the Underworld*, p.114

[15] ibid.

[16] *Njal's Saga*, (anon) http://omacl.org/Njal/

[17] Matthews, C, *King Arthur's Raid on the Underworld*, p.115

[18] Gerald of Wales, *The Journey Through Wales/The Description of Wales*, ed. Lewis Thorpe, (Penguin, Harmondsworth, 1978), p.134

[19] Meyer, Kuno & Alfred Nutt, *The Voyage of Bran Son of Febal* (2 vols London, David Nutt, 1895) vol 1, pp.32–4

Chapter 5 – The Three Illuminations

[1] O'hOgáin, Dáithí, *The Lore of Ireland*, (Boydell, Woodbridge, 2006), p.183

[2] ibid. p.429

[3] CM

[4] O'Donnacadh, Eoin, *Filid I Sanas Cormaic*, http://www.ucd.ie/ibp/MADissertations2009/Donnchadha.pdf, p.51

[5] CM

[6] Matthews, Caitlín & John, *Celtic Myth and Legend*, (Folio Society, London, 2002)

[7] Dooley, *Tales of the Elders of Ireland*, p.151

[8] Matthews, C. & J., *Celtic Myth and Legend*

[9] Cross, Tom Peete and Clark Harris Slover, *Ancient Irish Tales*, (Figgis, Dublin, 1936)

[10] Keeney, Bradford, *Shaking Medicine*, (Destiny Books, Rochester, 2007), p.155

[11] Pearson, Michael Parker, *The Archaeology of Death and Burial*, (History Press, 2003)

[12] Koch, *The Celtic Heroic Age,* p.9

[13] Matthews, C. & J., *Encyclopedia of Celtic Wisdom*

[14] ibid.

[15] Brown, Patrick, *The Revealing of the Táin Bó Cúailgne*, (http://www.paddybrown.co.uk/pdfs/The_Revealing_of_the_Tain_Bo_Cuailnge.pdf)

[16] Dooley, *Tales of the Elders of Ireland*, p.220

[17] ibid. p.6

[18] Matthews, C. & J., *Encyclopedia of Celtic Wisdom*

[19] Matthews, C., *The Elements of Celtic Tradition*

[20] Matthews, C. & J., *Encyclopedia of Celtic Wisdom*

Chapter 6 – Fate and Destiny

[1] CM

[2] Martin, *A Description of the Western Isles*

[3] Dooley, *Tales of the Elders of Ireland*

[4] Stokes, Whitley, *The Destruction of Da Derga's Hostel,* (P.F. Collier and Son Co., New York, 1909–14)

[5] ibid.

[6] CM

[7] Keating, Geoffrey, *Foras Feasa ar Éirinn: the History of Ireland*, D. Comyn and P.S. Dineen (eds.), (4 vols. Irish Texts Society, London, 1902-14.)

[8] CM

[9] Matthews, C. & J., *Encyclopedia of Celtic Myth and Legend*

[10] Davies, *The Mabinogion*

[11] Matthews, C & J, *Encyclopedia of Celtic Wisdom*

[12] Olmstead, Garret S., *The Gods of the Celts and the Indo-Europeans,* (Budapest, Archaeolingua Alapítvány, 1994), p.286

[13] Matthews, Caitlín, *The Spells of Women* in Ulrich Müller & Werber Wunderlich (eds.) *Verführer, Schurken, Magier* [Mitterlalter Mythen vol. 3] (UVK Verlagsgesellschaft, St Gallen, 2001)

[14] ibid.

[15] Matthews, C, *King Arthur's Raid on the Underworld*

[16] Geoffrey of Monmouth, *Vita Merlini*

[17] Matthews, C. & J., *Encyclopedia of Celtic Wisdom*

Chapter 7 – The Prophetic Vision

[1] Meyer, 1906, pp.8–11

[2] Koch, *The Celtic Heroic Age*, p.28

[3] CM

[4] Ellis, *The Druids,* p.244

[5] Davidson, *The Seer,* p.43

[6] Byrne, Francis, *Irish Kings and High Kings,* (Four Courts Press, Dublin, 2001), p.97

[7] Geoffrey, *Vita Merlini*

[8] CM

[9] Hemans, Felicia Dorothea, *The Poetical Works of Felicia Dorothea Hemans,* (Oxford University Press, London, 1914), pp.176–7

[10] *Book of Jonah*, Chapter 1

[11] Geoffrey of Monmouth, *Historia Regum Britainniae*

http://www.lib.rochester.edu/Camelot/geofhkb.htm

[12] ibid.

[13] Murray. James A. ed., *The Romance and Prophecies of Thomas of Erceldoune,* (Early English Text Society, London, 1875)

[14] ibid. p.lxxxvi

[15] Gerald of Wales, *The Journey Through Wales*

[16] CM

[17] Cross & Slover, *Ancient Irish Tales*

[18] Geoffrey, *Vita Merlini*

[19] CM

[20] CM

Chapter 8 – Omens and Divination

[1] Koch, *The Celtic Heroic Age,* p.37

[2] Aldhouse Green, Miranda, *Caesar's Druids*, (Yale University Press, New Haven, 2010), p.163

[3] Hooley-Jones, Cat. *Dreaming the Wild Man*, in *Sacred Hoop* no 70, 2010.

[4] Leupold, H. C. *Exposition of Genesis*, (Baker Book House, Grand Rapids, 1942), p.1081

[5] *Genesis* 44

[6] Matthews, C, *The Celtic Book of the Dead*

[7] CM

[8] Carmichael, *Ortha nan Gaidheal*, vol 2, CM trans.

[9] Ellis, *The Druids,* p.103

[10] Campbell, John Gregorson, *Superstitions of the Highlands and Islands of Scotland,* (James MacLehose, Glasgow, 1900), p.261

[11] Hunter, *The Occult Laboratory*, p.73

[12] Burnett, Charles, S.F. Arabic Divinatory Texts and Celtic Folklore: A Comment on the Theory and Practice of Scapulimancy in Western Europe, in *Cambridge Medieval Celtic Studies* vol 6., Winter 1983, pp.31–42 , p.33

[13] CM

[14] Matthews C. & J., *Encyclopedia of Celtic Wisdom*

[15] Wilby, *Cunning Folk*, p.69

[16] Welender, Richard, David J. Breeze, & Thomas Owen Clancy, eds., *The Stone of Destiny,* (Society of Antiquaries of Scotland, monograph series no 22, Edinburgh, 2003), p.105

[17] Breatnach, RA, *Marbhna fhearchair I haoil Chiarain, Eigse 3,* 1941–2, pp.165–85

[18] *Betha Colaim Chilla* (Life of Columcille) compiled by Maghnas O Domhnaill in 1532 ed. A. O'Kelleher and G. Schoepperle, (School of Celtic Studies, Dublin, 1994), trans. CM

[19] Carmichael, *Ortha nan Gaidheal*, vol 5, pp.287–8

[20] ibid. CM trans.

[21] ibid.

[22] ibid.

[23] ibid.

[24] MacKenzie, William, *Gaelic Incantations, Charms and Blessings of the Hebrides*, (Transactions of the Gaelic Society of Inverness, 1895)
http://www.archive.org/stream/gaelicincantati00mackgoog/gaelicincantati00mackgoog_djvu.txt

[25] ibid.

[26] ibid.

[27] ibid

[28] Matthews, C., *The Spells of Women*

[29] Ellis, *The Druids,* p.223

[30] Carey, *King of the Mysteries,* p.58

[31] O'Curry, *On the Manners and Customs of the Ancient Irish*

[32] Matthews, C., *King Arthur's Raid on the Underworld*

[33] O'Curry, *On the Manners and Customs of the Ancient Irish*

Chapter 9 – Visions of Wholeness

[1] CM

[2] Davies, *The Seer*

[3] CM

[4] Ellis, *The Druids,* p.168

[5] *Book of Leinster,* version ll, 4731ff, (http://www.maryjones.us/ctexts/leinster.html)

[6] Benozzo, Franceso. *Landscape Perception in Early Celtic Literature,* (Celtic Studies Publications, Aberwystwyth, 2004), trans. CM

[7] ibid.

[8] Matthews, C. & J., *Encyclopedia of Celtic Wisdom*

[9] Curtin, Jeremiah, *Myths & Folklore of Ireland*, (1890, http://www.surlalunefairytales.com/books/ireland/jeremiahcurtin.html)

[10] Matthews, J., *Taliesin: Shamanism and the Bardic Mysteries*

[11] Hunter, *The Occult Laboratory,* p.55

[12] Matthews, C., *King Arthur's Raid on the Underworld*

[13] CM

[14] Carey, *King of the Mysteries,* pp.90–91

[15] Kirk, *The Secret Common-Wealth*, p.56

[16] Geoffrey, *Vita Merlini*

[17] ibid.

[18] Matthews, J., *Taliesin: Shamanism and the Bardic Mysteries*

Glossary

The pronunciation of specialist Celtic terms in this index is given for guidance. The stress falls upon the syllable preceding the apostrophe.

an da shealleadh (un daa hall'la) – the two sights or 'the second sight'

anam (an'um) – soul

anim (an'um) – name

Annwfyn (An-uv'in) – the underworld

aos dana (eis daan'a) – the gifted people

awenyddion (awen-nith'ee-on) – seers or 'inspired ones'

beansí (pl. *mna-sí*) (ban'shee) – faery woman

Bendith y Mamau (Ben'deeth u Mam'eye) – 'the mothers' blessing' or faeries

brehon (be-re'un) – judge

co-choisiche (ko-ish'ika) – one who steps with you

coimimeadh (koim'ima) – co-walker

Coire Ernmae (Coi'ra Ern'mai) Cauldron of Vocation/Gifts

Coire Goriath (Coir'ra Gor'y-ath) Cauldron of Warming

Coire Sois (Coir'ra So'eesh) Cauldron of Great Knowledge

corrguinacht (corr-gwin'okt) – the crane's posture

crann beatha (crown bee'aha) – tree of life

crois-Taradh (cros tar'a) – 'cross measure' or stick divination

curadmír (coo'ra-meer) – the hero's portion

deiseal (jesh'al) – sunwise

Dichetul do Chennaib (Jee'het-ul do Hen'nib) – 'Invocation on the Finger's Ends'

eisteddfod (eye-steth'vod) – Welsh cultural festival

faith/faithí (Fawe/faw'ee) – seer

feis (fesh) – Irish cultural festival

feth-Fiadha (fe fee'aha) – invisible protection

filí (fil'ee) – vision poets

forcain (for'can) – to sing by rote

frith (free) – omen

frithir (Freer) – omen-seer

geis/geasa (gesh/gy'asa) – contracts of the soul

gléfiosa (glay fee'sa) – the bright knowledge, the light of wisdom

gruagach (groo'gach) – brownie

imbas (imm'bass) – inspiration, lit. 'kindling the fullness of knowledge'

mod (mod) – Scots Gaelic cultural festival

neldoracht (nel'do-ocht) – cloud divination

noinend (noi'nend) – ninefold curse

ofydd/ion (ov-ith'/of-ith'ee-on) – seers, prophets

ogham (og'am) – inscriptive strokes of writing upon bark-stripped twigs

ollamh (ol'lav) – the status of a doctorate

rosadach (ross'a-dok) – unlucky

sealbhach (shal'vak) – lucky

sí (shee) – faery

slinneachadh (slin'na-ca) – scapulimancy

suile coise (sooil'ya cosh'a) – eyes of the feet

suile méare (sooil'ya may'ra) – eyes of the fingers

taibhsear (taa'sher) – vision-seer

taidbsiu (tav'shoo) – apparition, spectre, vision

tarbh-feis (tar'ev fesh) – bull ceremony

Teinm Laegda (Chen'um Loi'je) – 'gnawing the pith or the poem'

Tír fa Thon (Cheer fa hon) – Land under Wave

Tuathal (too'a-hul) – widdershins

tuirgen (toor'gen) – circuit of lives

Bibliography

Aldhouse Green, Miranda, *Caesar's Druids*, Yale University Press, New Haven, 2010

Anon, *Njal's Saga*, http://omacl.org/Njal/

Benozzo, Franceso, *Landscape Perception in Early Celtic Literature*, Celtic Studies Publications, Aberwystwyth, 2004

Betha Colaim Chilla (Life of Columcille), compiled by Maghnas O Domhnaill in 1532 ed. A. O'Kelleher and G. Schoepperle, School of Celtic Studies, Dublin, 1994

Book of Leinster, version ll, 4731ff, (http://www.maryjones.us/ctexts/leinster.html)

Breatnach, R.A., *Marbhna fhearchair I haoil Chiarain*, Eigse 3, 1941–2, pp.165-85

Brown, Patrick, *The Revealing of the Táin Bó Cúailgne*, http://www.paddybrown.co.uk/pdfs/The_Revealing_of_the_Tain_Bo_Cuailnge.pdf

Burnett, Charles, S.F. Arabic Divinatory Texts and Celtic Folklore: A Comment on the Theory and Practice of Scapulimancy in Western Europe, in *Cambridge Medieval Celtic Studies* vol 6., Winter 1983, pp.31–42

Byrne, Francis, *Irish Kings and High Kings*, Four Courts Press, Dublin, 2001

Campbell, John Gregorson, *Witchcraft and Second Sight in the Highlands and Islands of Scotland*, James MacLehose, Glasgow, 1902

Campbell, John Gregorson, *Superstitions of the Highlands and Islands of Scotland*, James MacLehose, Glasgow, 1900

Carmichael, Alexander, *Ortha nan Gaidheal*, 6 vols, Oliver &
   Boyd, Edinburgh, 1971

Carey, John, *King of Mysteries: Early Irish Religious Writings*, Four
   Courts Press, Dublin, 2000

Chadwick, Nora K. *Imbas Forosnai*, Scottish Gaelic Studies, vol 4,
   part 2 Oxford University Press, Oxford, 1935

Corkery, Daniel, *The Hidden Ireland*, Gill and Macmillan, Dublin,
   1967

Cross, Tom Peete and Clark Harris Slover, *Ancient Irish Tales*,
   Figgis, Dublin, 1936

Curtin, Jeremiah, *Myths & Folklore of Ireland*, 1890,
   http://www.surlalunefairytales.com/books/ireland/jeremiah-
   curtin.html

Davidson, H.R. Ellis, *Gods and Myths of Northern Europe,*
   Penguin, London, 1964

Davidson, Hilda Ellis ed. *The Seer in Celtic and Other Traditions,*
   John Donaldson, Edinburgh, 1989

Davies, Sioned, *The Mabinogion*, Oxford University Press,
   Oxford, 2007

Dooley, Ann & Harry Roe, *Tales of the Elders of Ireland*, Oxford
   University Press, Oxford, 1999

Ellis, Peter Berresford, *The Druids*, Constable, London, 1994

Finlay, Ian, *Columba*, Richard Drew Publishing Ltd, Glasgow,
   1979

Geoffrey of Monmouth, *Historia Regnum Britanniae*
   http://www.lib.rochester.edu/Camelot/geofhkb.htm

Geoffrey of Monmouth, *Vita Merlini*,
   http://www.sacred-texts.com/neu/eng/vm/vmeng.htm

Gerald of Wales, *The Journey Through Wales/The Description of Wales*, ed. Lewis Thorpe, Penguin, Harmondsworth, 1978

Gregory, Lady Augusta, *Visions and Beliefs in the West of Ireland*, Colin Smythe Ltd., 1977

Hemans, Felicia Dorothea, *The Poetical Works of Felicia Dorothea Hemans*, Oxford University Press, London, 1914

Henderson, Lizanne & Edward J. Cowan, *Scottish Fairy Belief*, Tuckwell Press, Phantassie, 2001

Hooley-Jones, Cat, *Dreaming the Wild Man*, in *Sacred Hoop* no 70, 2010.

Hunter, Michael ed., *The Occult Laboratory: Magic, Science and Second Sight in Late 17th-Century Scotland*, Boydell Press, Woodbridge, 2001

Innes, Christian, *The Brahan Seer Trail*, Highland News Group, 2001

Keating, Geoffrey, *Foras Feasa ar Éirinn: the History of Ireland*, D. Comyn and P.S. Dineen (eds.) 4 vols. Irish Texts Society, London, 1902–14

Keeney, Bradford, *Shaking Medicine*, Destiny Books, 2007

Kirk, Robert, ed. Stewart Sanderson, *The Secret Common-Wealth*, D.S. Brewer, Cambridge, 1976

Koch, John T. & John Carey eds., *The Celtic Heroic Age: Literary Souces for Ancient Celtic Europe and Early Ireland and Wales*, Celtic Studies Publications, Malden, 1995

Lebor Gabala Erenn (5 vols), trans. R.A. Stewart, MacAlister, Irish Texts Society, Dublin, 1938–56

Leupold, H. C. *Exposition of Genesis*, Baker Book House, Grand Rapids, 1942

MacKenzie, Alexander, *The Prophecies of the Brahan Seer*, Constable, London, 1977

MacKenzie, William, *Gaelic Incantations, Charms and Blessings of the Hebrides*, Transactions of the Gaelic Society of Inverness, 1895 http://www.archive.org/stream/gaelicincantati00mack-goog/gaelicincantati00mackgoog_djvu.txt

Martin, Martin, *A Description of the Western Isles of Scotland*, http://www.appins.org/martin.htm

Matthews, Caitlín, T*he Celtic Book of the Dead*, Connections, London, 1992

Matthews, Caitlín, *Celtic Wisdom Box*, Connections, London, 2008

Matthews, Caitlín, *Celtic Wisdom Oracle: Ancestral Wisdom*, Watkins, London, 2011

Matthews, Caitlín, *Elements of Celtic Tradition*, Element, Shaftesbury, 1989

Matthews, Caitlín, *King Arthur's Raid on the Underworld*, Gothic Image, Glastonbury, 2008

Matthews, Caitlín, *Singing the Soul Back Home*, Connections, London, 1995

Matthews, Caitlín, *The Spells of Women* in Ulrich Müller & Werber Wunderlich (eds.) *Verführer, Schurken, Magier* (Mitterlalter Mythen vol. 3) UVK Verlagsgesellschaft, St Gallen, 2001

Matthews, Caitlín & John, *Encyclopedia of Celtic Myth & Legend*, Rider Books, London, 2011

Matthews, Caitlín & John, *Encyclopedia of Celtic Wisdom: A Celtic Shaman's Sourcebook*, Element Books, Shaftesbury, 1994

Matthews, Caitlín & John, *Celtic Myth and Legend*, Folio Society, 2002

Matthews, John, *Taliesin, Shamanism and the Bardic Mysteries in Britain and Ireland,* Aquarian, London, 1991

Lindahl, Carl, Lindow, John, McNamara, John, ed. *Medieval Folklore: an Encyclopedia of Myths, Legends, Tales, Beliefs, and Customs,* Oxford University Press, Oxford, 2002

Mees, Bernard, *Celtic Curses*, Boydell Presss, Woodbridge, 2009

Meyer, Kuno, ed. & trans., *Death Tales of the Irish Heroes,* Dublin, 1906

Meyer, Kuno trans. *Selections from Ancient Irish Poetry*, Constable & Co. Ltd., London, 1913

Meyer, Kuno & Alfred Nutt, *The Voyage of Bran Son of Febal,* David Nutt, 1895

Murray. James A. ed., *The Romance and Prophecies of Thomas of Erceldoune*, Early English Text Society, London, 1875

Neat, Timothy with John MacInnes, *The Voice of the Bard: Living Poets and Ancient Tradition in the Highlands and Islands of Scotland*, Canongate, Edinburgh, 1999

O'Curry, Eugene, *On the Manners and Customs of the Ancient Irish*, Williams and Norgate, 1873

O'Donnacadh, Eoin, *Filid I Sanas Cormaic*, http://www.ucd.ie/ibp/MADissertations2009/Donnchadha.pdf

O'hOgáin, Dáithí, *The Lore of Ireland*, Boydell, Woodbridge, 2006

Olmstead, Garret S., *The Gods of the Celts and the Indo-Europeans*, Archaeolingua Alapítvány, Budapest, 1994

Pearson, Michael Parker, *The Archaeology of Death and Burial*, History Press, 2003

Rees, Alwyn & Brinley, *Celtic Heritage*, Thames & Hudson, London, 1971

Sharkey, John, *The Medicine Tree: Traditional Healing in Wales from Pre-History to the Present*, Llanerch Press, Cribyn, 2008

Spence, Lewis, *Second Sight: Its History and Origins*, Rider, London, 1951

Stewart, R.J. *Robert Kirk: Walker Between Worlds*, Element Books, Shaftesbury, 1990

Stokes, Whitley, *The Destruction of Da Derga's Hostel*, P.F. Collier and Son Co., New York, 1909–14

Sutherland, Elizabeth, *Ravens and Black Rain,* Constable, London, 1985

Thesaurus Paeliohibernicus, ed. Whitley Stokes & John Strachan, Cambridge University Press, 1903

Welender, Richard, David J. Breeze, & Thomas Owen Clancy, eds., *The Stone of Destiny*, Society of Antiquaries of Scotland, monograph series no 22, Edinburgh, 2003

Wilby, Emma, *Cunning Folk and Familiar Spirits*, Sussex Academic Press, Brighton, 2005

Wilby, Emma, *The Visions of Isobel Gowdie: Magic, Witchcraft and Dark Shamanism in 17th century Scotland*, Sussex Academic Press, Eastbourne, 2010

Index